NOT
Buying It

Stop Overspending and Start Raising Happier, Healthier, More Successful Kids

BRETT GRAFF

Foreword by Dr. Gwen Wurm

SEAL PRESS

Seal Press
A Member of the Perseus Books Group
1700 Fourth Street
Berkeley, California
sealpress.com

ISBN: 978-1-58005-591-8

Library of Congress Cataloging-in-Publication Data:

Names: Graff, Brett, author.
Title: Not buying it : stop overspending and start raising happier, healthier, more successful kids / Brett Graff ; foreword by Dr. Gwen Wurm.
Description: Berkeley, California : Seal Press, 2015. | Includes bibliographical references.
Identifiers: LCCN 2015042207 | ISBN 9781580055918
Subjects: LCSH: Parents--Finance, Personal. | Child rearing--Economic aspects. | Families--Economic aspects. | Consumer education.
Classification: LCC HG179 .G7176 2015 | DDC 649/.1--dc23

Unless otherwise specified, the accounts of people in this book are fictional compilations of various actual events. Any familiarities reflect the author's work to incorporate situations faced by many, many families. Readers should conduct their own research and reach their own conclusions about the opinions described in this book. Publisher and author accept no responsibility for loss, injury, or inconvenience relating to the information and opinions in this book.

10 9 8 7 6 5 4 3 2 1

Cover design by Jason Ramirez
Interior design by Domini Dragoone
Printed in the United States of America
Distributed by Publishers Group West

This book is dedicated to the loving memory of Melvin H. Einhorn, who would have loved the job of proofreading every word.

Contents

Foreword

by Dr. Gwen Wurm

As a pediatrician, I am privileged to be a trusted voice in many families' lives—sometimes in unexpected ways. I am not sure when it happened, but in recent years, questions about breast-feeding began to morph into questions about what type or brand of breast pump. No longer was a car seat that passed safety standards good enough, but was the extra cushioning in "Brand Expensive" really better for a baby's delicate head? And mashing your own banana with a fork for baby's first food turned into the $150 Babycook Pro. As amusing as this is, I sense the struggles in parents' voices as they ask these questions. As children get older, it gets worse—my son's tennis coach said that Jeremy needed the $160 Babolat racket, and of course he couldn't possibly wear the sneakers he wears to school on the court. With all the money spent on lessons—and the driving to get him there—was it really the time to cut corners? Of course the medical bills from me wanting to kill him when he dragged the racket on the ground and jumped into puddles wearing the "special" sneakers were not figured into that equation.

Stop the craziness. This is the message of Brett Graff's *Not Buying It.* There is no requirement that in order to have healthy, happy, successful children, we have to spend our hard-earned dollars on the "right" stroller, educational toy, or private school. Study after study shows that it is not money that buys our children's success, but parents being parents. Being there to read to our children, encourage them on the playground, and stand and cheer at the school play. But all too often our fear gets in the way, and we spend money—money that we often don't have—on things that we have been told are "important."

Do not think that being a developmental pediatrician makes one immune to these messages. I remember going back and forth for weeks between buying the $40 big-box store bike for my four-year-old or the $200 Trek. Didn't I want my child to love bike riding? Didn't I want her to become athletic and develop a lifelong sport? And what about one day biking through Harvard Square? I decided to show her pictures of both. She wanted the purple one, and I was $160 the better. The bike had a great run for two years until she outgrew it and then it performed well for another two years for my niece. As for my daughter, she still loves to bike, and her bike is still purple. And according to Brett, that money is now worth close to $500, which might pay for the Thanksgiving vacation airfare from college (assuming she doesn't use it to go to Cancún with friends).

In *Not Buying It,* Brett proves that all the stuff we're buying does not come with guarantees and also can wind up putting our kids at a disadvantage. She shows us that *not* spending money is the way to go. Economic stability is its own reward; protecting our kids from debt is one of the best gifts we can give. But as a doctor, parent, and child advocate, I find that *Not Buying It* offers more than advice on saving money—it offers freedom from the fear that marketers, friends, schools, and even other parents are instilling in our vulnerable brains. This book has the empowering information we can use to make our own smart choices. Brett gives us the tools to analyze the claims that bombard us from the media, teachers, and other parents. She takes on the companies, the advertisers, the "experts" who tell us what to do to ensure our children's success. She challenges their assumptions and provides hard data to say that we are being misled, and that there could be lifelong consequences. Because not only do we get scared by the advertising that tells us that our child's future is at stake, but our children get scared too.

It is both heartbreaking and infuriating to see preschoolers spending long hours in the car, being driven to $200 math classes where they'll do worksheets instead of playing happily, counting flower petals, in their own backyards. Or walking into the exam room to find a patient of any age—but especially the babies—hypnotized by an $800 electronic device instead of singing with mom. Families in our practice routinely move to other counties for a bigger home that's far away from the father's job. I hope the kids are happier having their own rooms. But I bet they would trade it for having Dad read a bedtime story.

It starts prenatally—remember the fad of headphones placed on pregnant women's bellies in the hope that playing classical music to fetuses would lead to math geniuses? For every pound of baby, the typical family buys at least one hundred pounds of stuff. And we research, debate, and fret about each purchase. Companies pummel us with ads about what it takes to make our babies college-ready: Provide them with foreign language phonemes and teach them sign language, or else they will be behind before they ever learn to walk. Don't cheap out on the $30 video that may start their superstar on the way to Stanford. The message of *Not Buying It* is that little if any of this is true. It is time for us to go back to following our hearts and not parenting by credit card.

So what do we really want for our children? I believe that all of us want our children to be happy, healthy, self-supporting (yes, that is important) adults who can form loving lifelong relationships. Parents who listen, laugh, allow kids to fall, and are there to put on the bandages can help make that happen. It takes time and energy and lots of love—and you can't buy it on an installment plan for $19.95 a month. By writing *Not Buying It*, Brett gives us permission to get off the roller coaster and to relax and enjoy our children. There is no better way to spend a Sunday afternoon.

Raising children is an adventure—and we can't buy our way out of this one.

Introduction

Spending money to keep up with our friends is so pre-recession. Everyone knows emergency funds are the new extravagance. But when it comes to raising kids, we're still overspending big time, hemorrhaging money by mistaking luxuries for necessities and doling out more dollars than we save. And why? Because we're afraid that cheaping out means our kids will fall behind in school, sports, or social activities. And in a high-pressure parenting climate, there is no room for error; academic admissions are competitive and—down the road—jobs are scarce. We're terrified our kids won't get into college and will even later wind up homeless. Or worse, wind up living in our homes.

Like any severe panic, this anxiety disrupts logic, and we experience a flight-or-fight reaction. Flight, we've learned, is impossible—who would check the homework?—and so we're left to fight. Ammunition is expensive and includes high-performance sneakers, toddler learning programs and teen music lessons, private schools, allegedly organic everything, designer clothes. Where aren't we putting our money? In the very financial foundations that really can launch kids into greatness. There are two unfortunate consequences. First, we're going broke. And second, we're messing up our kids in almost every possible way. Admit it, you do this or you see this but probably both: parents spending money on kid-improvements such as singing lessons, private schools, and fancy lacrosse sticks not because they're rich but because they're scared. Or competitive. Or vulnerable. In any case, they're simply unaware that these things are unnecessary in reaching the supposed goal of raising children who achieve their fullest potential.

I, for one, want my money back. For all the stupid things I bought for my daughter because I was afraid *not* buying them would mean she wouldn't be as smart, as athletic, as healthy as she could be. In my defense, I didn't want her to have any disadvantages. If I could get my money back for just three simple things, it would be these: a heavy, smooth-ride stroller with huge wheels that I never used ($600); a bunch of educational toys, some of which were eventually recalled ($500); and the homeopathic medicine that didn't make her feel better ($1,200). And I could take that $2,300 and put it into a stock fund earning 7 percent. (Warren Buffett says we should expect that's the long-term return, even though rates have been higher.)[1] Today, some thirteen years later, that money would be worth $5,542. So I consider myself down by that very amount.

Yes, after these unfortunate purchases, I started professionally researching the relationship between behavior and economics and learned that economists are wrong: They assume humans are rational shoppers. This assumption is particularly flawed when those humans happen to be parents. All of us, on the other hand, are economists in a job that requires making decisions about how to best allocate time and money. We are *all*, I say, Home Economists. And we work at it every day.

And right now, we're working under hysterical conditions. Take my friend—we'll call her "Beth"—who spent $300 having her son's tennis racket restrung at home in Florida and then overnighted to his sleep-away camp in Maine. Beth's behavior was in response to an unde-sirable outcome that *is* imaginable. But only because Beth imagined it.

Initially responding to her son's tennis racket complaints over the phone with the concern of a parent who is well-trained at changing the subject—Did he have a girlfriend? Did he like the camp food?—Beth began listening when the kid mentioned an upcoming tournament. Beth then thought about his winning, and how perhaps it would help him enjoy his summer more, making that high-priced camp tuition worth every penny. That would be nice, she thought. It would jus-tify camp, not to mention his weekly tennis lessons. Winning—as she thought more about it—could give him new confidence, attract girls, change the summer and maybe, just maybe, his life. Wow. This tournament could be really great. But wait. Those damn strings. They could make him lose. Would the opposite happen? Would he be sad? What would be the lasting effects? Would he eventually lose friends and later—give or take a few decades—career opportunities?

Well, if you can buy your child confidence and career opportu-nities for $300, a new tennis racket suddenly seems an essential pur-chase, like schoolbooks or a winter jacket.

But this logic is false. For starters, statistics prove that in every professional sport where both players have sponsorships providing unlimited equipment, *someone* typically loses.

And this line of reasoning isn't limited to Beth or her son or even sports in general. We're all scared our child's missteps will be our fault because we didn't buy the new equipment, tuitions, voice lessons, learning toys, private school, organic sleepwear, private acupunctur-ists, brand-name sneakers. But here's the thing: If we can avoid even half of the biggest fear-induced expenses—from toys to schools to les-sons to the house we feel are the tickets to American happiness—we can save ourselves not only sometimes $1 million but also an enor-mous amount of emotional aggravation.

Today, parents are spending 100 percent more money on our children since the 1970s, according to a report from University of

Pennsylvania.[2] The richest among us have simply ramped up the dollar amounts. The poorest are maintaining the same levels but using a bigger portion of income. For example, while the lowest-earning domiciles used to spend 4.48 percent of their incomes on their kids, they're now spending 13.79 percent.

We all feel pressure. It's an arms race. We have to calm down. Because whether we have piles of money or very little, the notion of letting fear rule our spending decisions is completely messing everything up, most notably our kids. Because this spending can very possibly result in the opposite of what we intend, causing emotional scars and irreparably cracking the financial foundations that really can launch these little guys into greatness.

Never has any organization in the history of this country asked its job applicants to please list on a resume the toys or learning programs used during their toddler years. Organizations do frequently, however, ask for the names of the colleges or graduate schools attended.

Stop it.

I know what you're thinking: The Mandarin Chinese toy will eventually contribute to college acceptances and scholarships. But there is no link. Only a predictable lag between the introduction of a new learning toy and the proof it sets back your child's intellect. Yes: Sets. It. Back. There's also a short time interval between you purchasing the product and you donating it to Goodwill. Time flies when you're wasting money.

In this book, I'll show you how to end the fear-induced overspending and instead practice effective money-saving parenting habits. For example, the most productive learning activities for your baby are free. The opposite, however, is true for your eighteen-year-old. College is practically guaranteed to improve the life of your child and happens to be very expensive. If you want your kid to go, you must on the way home from the baby's birth learn to ignore the educational toys and start funding a Section 529 plan. Unlike giving your money to a store and never seeing it again, in college savings plans you can watch it grow. That's good because it takes a long time to save up some $400,000, which is the projected cost of a four-year public, out-of-state college education for the fall of 2033.[3]

Money is critical for raising kids, that's for sure. But rather than make emotionally charged purchases that destroy us financially, we have to direct our dollars toward building Rock-Solid Foundations. We need concrete blocks of financial security to support our families. They consist of college funds and emergency accounts, insurance policies, reasonable home purchases, and reliable medical care.

If money's so critical, am I saying parenting is easier if you're rich? Of course it is!

But you're not guaranteed to raise better children. There is no correlation between the amount of money spent on a child and the quality of person she becomes. In fact, making fear-based purchases can physically or emotionally mess up rich kids and upper-middle class kids as quickly as it can middle-class and poor kids. And in 2012, there were over 265,000 toy-related visits to hospital emergency rooms, according to the Federal Trade Commission.[4] We can thank something called a Nap Nanny for five infant deaths and a fancy video monitor for one strangulation. Narcissistic personalities—which ultimately can cause depression—are becoming more common among our kids, to the tune of some 30 percent.[5] And the coaches and private music teachers for which we pay big money play a huge role, with their lavish (and high-priced) praise.

You can certainly buy a huge, gated mansion with a bedroom for each child, but a Danish study proves that kids who walk or bike to school—sometimes from city apartments—concentrate better for over four hours after arriving. Sibling bedroom-sharing, meanwhile, has been linked to feelings of security. You can spend a lifetime on organic, well, everything, if you like, but some products labeled organic have been found to contain dangerous chemicals that can truly harm your child. Which reminds me: Be careful about natural remedies, fancy private schools, and overly groomed neighborhoods reeking of affluence. I'll show you how their promises are sometimes empty and their costs—when you count missed opportunities—can be much higher than the visible price tag.

Then there's plain, old materialism. None of us considers ourselves to be overly concerned with possessions. But even passed on inadvertently—materialism is usually taught to kids by parents—a person's race for sneakers or brand names in effect causes insecurity, a poor sense of self, and general unhappiness.

Forget it.

Good news for every income level: The most effective ways to groom our kids for greatness, happiness, and success are usually low-cost or free. They're usually what you think of in moments of calm—when you're not terrified of having the only preschooler not fluent in French or worrying that the dye used to color your bed sheets is causing cancer or that your high schooler won't become a college athlete or will turn into a social outcast for not wearing the sneaker du jour.

The parenting methods that truly achieve what many of us are trying to buy are the most wholesome, most logical, and most effective ways to raise kids. You see, God or the universe or evolution—take your pick—provided human beings with built-in mechanisms to make our babies smarter and our kids more secure. What makes an athletic star or a pianist? Practice. What makes kids happy? Positive life experiences. Parents can turn practically any activity into a teachable moment that imparts math, vocabulary, and reading skills while you're supermarket shopping, cuddling, crafting, cooking, and putting kids to bed.

Natural and effective parenting involves hard work but also putting your babies, toddlers, kids, and teens first. In fact, this book will spell out the research proving that the time-tested techniques that truly do advance children cannot be replaced with money-purchased surrogates that can instead be complete failures.

I know we've all made many of these mistakes, but I for one am determined not to repeat them. My kids aren't grown; they still have a chance! Unless yours are adults, they do, too. This book will benefit your babies, toddlers, elementary schoolers, junior high schoolers, and high schoolers. All kids are clearly destined for greatness. They are! Your child really is amazing. Let's keep that kid on the right track. Let's save in the right ways, spend when necessary, and ensure that this kid gets the truly effective support he or she needs.

You'll see that effective parenting isn't necessarily store-bought. I am here to show you the evidence proving we can't buy for our kids with the intention of solving our problems, because their expensive outcomes are not guaranteed to be great. We should instead focus on the scenarios that really can buckle a family: Losing our jobs and not having emergency funds to support us as we get back on our feet. The head of household dying without life insurance or becoming injured and unable to work but not having disability insurance. Your kid getting into Harvard University and having to tell her she can't go because you can't afford the tuition—or, just as bad, paying for it but having nothing left over for retirement. You're scared now, but stop—because I'll show you how to make sure none of this happens.

In this book, you'll learn to save—possibly $1 million, or even more—after you see that fear-based spending contributes to materialism, stress, insecurity, and possibly very poor health. And you'll be introduced to the free or low-cost alternative that's more reliable, more wholesome, and more effective for promoting the very kind of achievement other parents are busy trying to buy for their children. Then, I'll show you how to use the money left over to build a Rock-Solid Financial Foundation that will continue to expand and make you richer over time, and also really and truly catapult your kid into greatness. I'll show you how to fund a college savings plan so your child can choose the school she *wants* (not the one offering the most financial aid). I'll show you that an emergency fund can ensure your athlete or actor will pursue his hobby under any financial circumstances. You'll also learn to choose the right public or private school and save for retirement—because otherwise, you're just a big, fat financial burden on the very people you're so busy grooming for greatness.

I'm not saying that private violin lessons or a pair of designer sneakers will screw up your kid. You may still, after reading, buy expensive sneakers and private coaches and fancy schools and costly strollers. But you'll do it because you want to. Not because you have to. You won't feel the fear of *not* buying those things.

CHAPTER ONE

Starting Out

choose
COLLEGE SAVINGS
OVER COMMERCIAL SPENDING

Save Estimated $6,428.19

The Stuff You'll Skip

Stroller: $650.00

Bottle warmer: $39.99

Wipes warmer: $29.00

Infant sleeper set: $129.00

Video baby monitor: $239.99

Stroller fan: $19.99

Play yard netting: $8.99

Stroller seat cover: $59.99

Diaper stacker: $24.99

Infant swing: $159.99

Infant bouncer: $249.99

Air purifier: $169.99

Stationary entertainer: $99.99

Classical baby art DVD: $6.99

Baby TV Musical Instruments DVD: $5.99

Classical Baby Dance DVD: $6.99

Total Cash Outlay: $1,901.87

Total Invested Savings after 18 Years: $6,428.19

The editors of a popular baby website have compiled for their large community of moms-to-be a list of the best strollers around. One such model reminded the editorial panel of a transformer, and the group collectively gushed about how you can even charge your cell phone with this bad boy. This stroller, like nearly all the editors' picks—including one you can carry on your back (which makes one wonder why you wouldn't just carry your baby)—costs more than $800.

This may sound old-fashioned, but I think it's perfectly fine to charge your cell phone at home.

Keep in mind, those baby website editors—and also their readers who are presumably weeks away from having babies—have every reason to be excited. Becoming a parent is the most thrilling and transforming of all life's events. Not to mention the one that involves the most responsibility. We're going to be in charge of tiny, defenseless human beings. And we know it's our job to protect, nurture, and safeguard our children the best we can. We're ready to do anything and we're prepared to *buy* anything. Just tell us what we need.

That's the attitude that makes a profit-seeking industry salivate: customers who are emotional, inexperienced, terrified, and deeply committed to the cause for which they're shopping. All together, in the United States we bought about $5.8 billion worth of baby stuff online[1] in 2013 and about $11.9 billion in stores[2] that same year, according to research from IBISWorld. We fill our carts with infant merchandise we truly believe is critical for the child's survival. Never mind that the human race has survived some two hundred thousand years *without* cell phone–charging strollers.

Not only will our kids endure, but also we can in some cases do a better job of parenting if we calm down long enough to stop adding things to our carts. Yes, we'll need to buy for our babies—items such as cribs, car seats, clothes, and of course strollers. But while considering our choices, we have to remember that we don't need every single product on the market. What's more, the most expensive versions with the fanciest features are not—under any circumstances—safer. They're not more educational. They won't make our infants happier.

No matter what we buy, all of it is guaranteed in a matter of two years (maybe three) to evolve into garbage, as your child grows. If you spend too much money on what will soon be a Salvation Army donation—even if you can well afford it today—you likely are taking from your child other things that can really improve her life later on.

Nursery Ready
CRIBS

You must buy a crib, and if there's a purchase we promise is for short-term use, it's a bed that by design creates a barrier between the bathroom and your future toilet-trained toddler. This is not an item you will have forever. For now, the one and only feature your infant crib must have is a manufacture date of June 28, 2011, or later. Do not buy your crib at a thrift store; do not accept a hand-me-down. Current safety standards apply *only* to cribs made after that date. Before that day, the Consumer Product Safety Commission announced forty-six recalls of more than eleven million cribs because they had the potential to strangle or suffocate children.

That's exactly the kind of statistic that can cause a new parent to panic and buy the most expensive crib available—for safety's sake. Thing is, spending more money on a crib does not buy you a safer crib. Some very high-priced brands have rushed to return money to customers because they turned out to have dangerous entrapment and suffocation hazards. In October 2010, for example, Ethan Allan recalled its drop-side cribs selling for between $550 and $900 after the company learned the drop side could detach, thanks to malfunctioning hardware.[3] One baby became entrapped and two fell out. In July 2010, Pottery Barn recalled its $600 drop-side crib after thirty-six reported problems.[4] There were also recalls of lower-priced models. The general problem here was a new drop-side feature that made it easy to reach infants but was discovered to be dangerous. While new federal standards ban drop sides—while demanding slats be stronger, mattresses more supportive, and hardware more durable (find the standards at www.cpsc.gov)—one thing is still true: More money doesn't buy you a safer crib. First, these strict standards apply to every crib for sale in America. That means the $895 Vanessa sold by baby-store-to-the-stars, Bellini, and the $159 Graco sold by website-to-the-unshowered, Amazon.com, have been subject to the same inspection process.

And second, when you look at recent product deficiencies—even after the government called for stricter standards—it was two high-end and two mid-priced lines that were found to trap and suffocate babies. In August of 2014 a Franklin & Ben Mason model—retailing for $700 in stylish colors such as "weathered grey" and "rustic brown"—was recalled for the potential to trap babies.[5] And that same year, the slats and spindles (the very reason you buy a crib, it's worth mentioning) of the $800 Oeuf Sparrow cribs were detaching.[6] Parents who chose the most reasonably priced cribs fared better in more ways than one.

BABY MONITORS

To protect against the dangers posed at bedtime you're likely ready to invest in a baby monitor, *big time*. The temptation is to choose a model high tech enough to notify you when—if this is even available—your baby drifts throughout the sleep cycles. We're talking about the kind of equipment employed by spies and secret service agents. If safety's at stake, who cares what it costs?

Video monitors—some costing $350—make it possible to watch real-time footage of your baby, even sending the action to your smartphone. Others have cameras that can pan to show the rest of the room.

They all typically allow two-way communication, so you can even talk to your baby from wherever you happen to be.

But what if the real price is compromised security for your entire family? Because if your camera is hacked—and let's be very clear, your camera can be hacked—there will be some unwelcome company in your baby's room. Adam and Heather Schreck told Fox News they were sleeping in their home when they heard a man yelling, "Wake up baby, wake up," at their ten-month old daughter.[7] Heather picked up her cell phone to check the wireless video monitor in the baby's room and saw the camera was panning, seemingly by itself. Adam raced in and, when he entered, the camera rotated from the baby and aimed itself at him, and *he* became the target of the hacker's obscenities.

Even before this story and others like it hit the news, Jeff Weinsier of Miami ABC affiliate WPLG reported on air that he set up a generic video baby monitor receiver in his news vehicle and drove around local neighborhoods.[8] The receiver picked up footage of babies in house after house, crib after crib, and monitor after monitor. Passing by some homes he saw sleeping babies, driving by other homes he saw empty cribs. Turns out, watching other people's babies is even easier than taking candy from them.

If you're using a monitor that wirelessly uses the Internet to send video to your phone or mobile device, then you may at some point access a public Internet connection, say, at a coffee shop or an airport, explains Michael Peros, chief technical officer for Bugged.com. It then takes only simple equipment—in some cases a download—for a hacker to nudge himself between the router and your phone, where he intercepts all the information being sent to you—without you even *knowing*. Not only will the hacker see everything you see—your baby, for starters and also, say, your emails about when you'll be away from your baby—but he has access to all the information stored on your device, including your calendar. Putting it all together: He knows what your kid looks like *and* when you will be on a business trip.

Even monitors that access password-protected wireless Internet connections are not safe, says Peros. Our passwords are easily cracked in seconds by a simple download, usually because they're pretty short. "The internet was created for sharing information," says Peros. "Anyone who says 'it's secure' is lying."

There are video monitors that don't use the Internet; those are the ones that Miami reporter Weinsier was able to access from his truck. How? Because all baby monitors operate on the same frequency, says Peros. The Federal Communications System demands it; otherwise the monitors would bleed into the frequencies used by burglar alarms or cell phones. And monitors are open and ready to connect. Weinsier demonstrated this frequency phenomenon to the mothers he invited outside after discovering he could see their kids. Most of them vowed to shut their own monitors off for good, wondering out loud how many times they'd been watched themselves. These women were mostly worried about walking around half dressed or breast-feeding, which if you ask me, says a lot about their fine parenting, strong marital relationships, and overall sanity. (I for one shiver at the thought of a stranger listening to my uncensored dialogue.)

We also shouldn't bother skipping the wireless in favor of cords. Summer Infant had to recall two models of baby monitors with electrical cords after two kids strangled themselves.[9] One was a ten-month girl from Washington, DC, whose camera had been placed on the top of the crib rail. And another was a six-month old boy from Conway, South Carolina, whose monitor had been placed on the changing table attached to the crib. Also, a twenty-month-old boy from Pittsburgh, Pennsylvania, was freed in time, but was found in his crib with the camera cord wrapped around his neck.

Another option for nightly baby espionage is a monitor that records your baby's movements. But again, those darn cords. The ones attached to the Angelcare Movement and Sound Monitor strangled two babies who pulled the cords from under their mattresses and into their cribs.[10]

The good news is that the traditional baby monitors—the audio kind made by companies including Graco, Safety 1st, Summer Infant, and Angelcare—are still for sale in stores, starting at about $13.99. Monitors are typically handy at night, when we're sleeping and wouldn't otherwise hear our baby's cries, nature's alerts to the fact that the child needs something. Maybe it's a changing, maybe a feeding, perhaps a little conversation—babies are fanciful with their late-night requests. But it's the noise—the audio—that would notify you. Not the video.

Would a streaming video of the kid help you sleep better? News flash: New parents are not afforded the luxury of sleep. But even so, the answer is no, probably not. A video offers some convenience in that you can look up at the monitor while eating peanut butter in the kitchen instead of getting up and walking into your kid's room. But even if your journey to that crib happens to be particularly arduous, it's also likely productive. Who is the better cop: the one in the security office with her feet up, glancing occasionally at a monitor? Or the one checking things out in person, shining a flashlight and peeking around? Wouldn't that cop be more likely to notice something awry? Perhaps the crib sheets are too loose or someone left the window open?

BATH SEATS

One Step Ahead tells you on every page of its website that the company is "helping you raise happy, healthy kids." And yes, that's true in that the company designs and manufactures products that can—if used properly—be very helpful. That's what the slogan means. But, their engineers are not in your home, lending a hand at bath time. And the products do not operate on their own. And in June 2013, the company's Chelsea & Scott bath seats were recalled for failing to meet safety standards.[11] In fact, from late 2012 to 2013, over thirteen models of bath seats—including those by Dream on Me[12] and Thermobaby[13]—were found to tip over.

Let's be clear: Bath seats themselves will not harm our children. On the contrary, bath seats allow us to wash the kids with two hands. But a super high-end bath seat with thick suction cups, plush cushions, and play toys may give an adult the kind of false sense of security that lets her rush to shut off the oven or check a text. More than 471 babies less than twenty-four months old died in bathtubs between 2006 and 2010, according to a report from the Consumer Product Safety Commission.[14] Another 191 kids were injured. The most common reason, says the report, is that the children were left alone while caregivers figured for just one moment they could tend to other activities. A strong and expensive bath seat would not have saved them. An on-site adult, on the other hand, would have.

You know better than that, you're thinking. You'd never leave your baby unattended. But is anyone else going to bathe your child? Grandparents? Aunts? Babysitters? Are you 100-percent-super-triple-quadruple sure?

Today bath seat standards are stricter. They're supposed to tip less easily. But the Number One change is in the size of the label—it's bigger—warning you to watch your kid. We can spend as much money as we like, but (1) we need a human adult in that room at all times, (2) we'll still toss it in five months—shorter than your pregnancy—and (3) like cribs, all bath seats must adhere to the same federal safety standards.

Car Seats

If you want to protect your child from death, then car seats are totally the way to go. When it comes to automobile accidents, car seats reduce the risk of death to infants by 71 percent, says the Centers for Disease Control and Prevention, and reduce the risk of death to toddlers by 54 percent.[15]

Heather Darby, child passenger and safety coordinator at the Minnesota Department of Public Safety, says to consider two things without fail. First, she recommends buying the best-fitting seat for our children—height and weight limits for each model are listed on the box. And second, we absolutely have to choose the seat we find easiest to install.[16]

The most expensive car seat won't provide more safety, though it may cause confusion that could be dangerous, says Darby. See, regardless of whether a car seat costs $50 or $500, all makes and models are required by federal law to follow the same strict safety standards. Though more cash might get you thicker padding that could come in handy on day-long drives, these models may also have additional seat belt glides or seat belt locks that make installation more difficult. There's one detail to which you must attend before your car seat can perform its life-saving mission: making certain it's properly installed in the car. You wouldn't pull a television from a box, stick it on a table and expect it to work—no matter how much you paid. Same thing with your car seat.

Yet still, the CDC found over 72 percent of car seats were misused in a way that could be expected to increase a child's risk of injury during a crash.[17] There are many degrees of ineptitude here, so we'll start at the very beginning: Simply tossing it in the car without any proper and secure attachments or—it's hard to believe we're going here—neglecting to strap in the child is equivalent to not having a seat at all.

But even minor missteps can be deadly. If the seat belt isn't locked or the lock isn't secure, the car seat will swing wildly in a crash. If we route the seat belt through the wrong tracks, which can happen if, say, the car seat is convertible from rear- to front-facing and maintains distinct routes for each installation, the car seat will not work to its maximum potential.

If your car was built before 1996, then you will need some extra features, most notably a contraption called a "lock off." This sets the seat belt into lock mode, so in the event of a crash, the car seat doesn't jar in any direction. Cars constructed after that year are required to have seat belts that lock automatically, which is perhaps something you—like me—already learned when yours for no apparent reason constricted around your neck. The way it's *supposed* to work, however, is that after pulled out to its longest capability and then released at the desired length, the belt should lock back into place. If your car was built after 1996, you might want to implement this latch system, which locks the belt in place.

Here's the good news: Personalized help installing your car seat is completely free. You can ensure that any seat is tightly secured by going to almost any hospital, fire station, or police station. What's more, Safekids.org hosts more than eight thousand safety inspection events across the country. Their technicians take a four-day course and are trained in car seat installation.

There are also some tips from officials to consider. Keep your child in a rear-facing seat until age two, says American Academy of Pediatrics.[18] Your child should not shift more than one inch side to side or out from the seat. The harness material around the baby should be snug. If you can pinch it, it's too loose. The retainer clip should be at the child's armpit level, not higher or lower. It also helps to follow state laws about seats, which is not only safe but also cost-effective, as there are fines.

The Laws of Car Seat Safety

The decision to reverse a rear-facing seat or switch to a booster is one governed by state law. The Governors Highway Safety Association (www.ghsa.org) lists the restraint required by ages and weights on its Child Passenger Safety Laws page: www.ghsa.org/html/stateinfo/laws/childsafety_laws.html.

Feeding Frenzy

I would as a personal opinion say that money for infant formula is well spent, but economists and researchers and doctors—essentially the entire free world—point to the benefits of breast-feeding. The National Resources Defense Council even has a handout, reminding us all that mother's milk strengthens a baby's immune system, reduces ear infections, and protects against allergies, dental cavities, and cancer.[19]

There are also some pretty significant economic benefits, according to the NRDC. Formula costs $800 a year. And what's more, over the long term, one group of formula-fed infants had $68,000 in health care costs over a six-month period compared to an equal number of nursing babies, which had only $4,000 of similar expenses. Formula feeding also requires buying a collection of products—bottles, bottle cleaners, bottle warmers, and nipples, many of which you'll never use—which is not a fact from the NRDC but a fact nonetheless (trust me). And it's only fair to mention that breast-feeders with jobs will need those things too, plus a pump.

Breast-feeding wins by a mile (we get it, we get it), but if we do decide to perform the unthinkable—introducing to our babies' systems the manufactured nutrients in infant formula—we'll have to pick a brand to serve. You can seek out prices in stores if you happen to feel compelled to comparison shop. But these companies don't give you that kind of time. They're waiting for you at the hospital with samples, hoping to get you at the start of this journey and stick with you until the toddler end.

The good news is that formula produced in this country is going to be a fine blend of milk solids and chlorides and other essentials. The better news? If you wanted to switch to a less expensive brand, that would be very well too. The Food and Drug Administration carefully regulates infant formula, setting minimum amounts of twenty-nine nutrients and maximum amounts for nine of those nutrients. Although manufacturers might vary in their formula recipes, says the

Mayo Clinic on its website,[20] the FDA requires that all formulas contain the recommended amount—and no more than the maximum amount—of nutrients that infants need.

Raise Them Better for Less

In the unlikely event the theme of the past few pages wasn't as noticeable as a baby food stain on a new silk shirt: All baby products are required to adhere to the same federal standards regardless of the price stamped on the package. That means selecting the least expensive products—even when doing so for exactly that reason—will not put your child's sleep patterns or automobile safety at risk. It does not make you less of a parent. It does not mean you don't care. It means you *may* not own the occasional unnecessary bells and whistles. It means you will have more money for more important things. (I have a whole book of them here.)

Thing is, even if those features seem attractive—perhaps even critical—in the store, they could make you miserable at home. Researchers from Washington University in St. Louis found that shoppers who chose more expensive, complicated products were more likely to later have buyer's remorse.[21] After a series of four experiments, they learned buyers were overwhelmed with all those features. When it comes time to install them, they really just wished the product would perform the basic function they bought it to do in the first place.

The true gauge of parent wealth might be not the crib the kid owns but the number of words she's taught. Betty Hart and Todd Risley in 1992 visited homes of families across socioeconomic backgrounds to examine the conversations between parents and children.[22] They found that wealthier parents spoke more frequently and more positively to their children. As a result babies on welfare heard about 616 words per hour, while those from working-class families heard around 1,251 words per hour, and those from professional families heard roughly 2,153 words per hour. By the time the kids were three years old, there was a thirty-million-word gap between the kids whose parents were professionals and those on welfare. After follow-up investigations when the kids reached third grade—ages nine and ten—the researchers discovered those who heard more words as babies had made greater academic advances in critical areas such as vocabulary, language development, and reading comprehension. They quickly concluded that the kids who start behind will stay behind.

Parents can do a lot for free. Speaking to our babies is a good start. But we can also accelerate the vocab-building process by including the baby's name in those sentences, says Heather Bortfeld, a developmental psychology professor at University of Connecticut.[23] Babies recognize their own names at about 4.5 months and can then start to use them as anchors that will put other words into context, says Bortfeld. Think about it this way: When you hear people speaking a language you don't understand—Ukrainian, perhaps—it sounds like a stream of sounds that doesn't seem to break into words, she explains. But if you happened to recognize one single word, say, *weekend*, then you can start to figure out the meaning of surrounding words.

It works the same way with babies who don't understand most of the language but can hone in on their names and words such as *Mommy*. In a series of experiments, Bortfeld found that six-month-old babies could recognize new vocabulary words that had been anchored to their own names, but not new ones anchored to another name, even though they had heard the two vocabulary words equally as often. They also listened longer to conversations that contained their names, proving they could more fluently process those words (and are as egotistical as we are).

The wonderful news is not only is it in your interest to skip apps and screens and toys, but also you have someone new to listen to all your brilliant remarks in the event your spouse is tiring of them. To teach your child new words, simply speak to her. And you don't have to be there all day. If you're dashing off to work, explain to the kid over your quiet breakfast of eggs and juice—hahaha, just kidding—scream to your child over your shoulder (while racing to locate a clean shirt) some of the activities she'll be doing that day. Tell him what you'll be having for dinner. Good news: Without the ability to speak back, the kid can't complain if you change the menu. (Just don't be surprised if he one day excitedly exclaims, "filet mignon" at the sight of a Chinese takeout container.)

When we get tired of speaking to our babies, we should just ignore them, a practice that also turns out to be highly educational. That's because infants as young as four months of age who play solo with an adult nearby will learn to think creatively and problem-solve, says the American Academy of Pediatrics.[24] Presumably, your home has a floor, which means you're already equipped for this activity. Floors offer bountiful opportunities for exploration, making them superior to restrictive playpens, high chairs, or walkers, says Dr. Gwen Wurm, an assistant professor at University of Miami Miller School of Medicine, who is board-certified in developmental, behavioral, and general pediatrics. While the kid is down there on the floor, toss him a Tupperware container—it's a little-known fact, but Tupperware products are highly celebrated in the medical community—and perhaps a wooden spoon. You have then provided your child with tools proven to build cognitive development. These items will help build physical and mental strength, says Dr. Wurm. First, by playing with safe objects and interacting with their natural environments, babies are learning cause and effect. They find out that holding something the wrong way will cause it to fall. They understand that lifting something heavy is often impossible and that putting something in your mouth means you'll have something in your mouth. All groundbreaking discoveries. You can't possibly move on to Mandarin Chinese or advanced calculus without having made these first. Learning starts here, people.

Floor play is also good exercise. Think about it: If you've spent your entire life lying down on your back, guzzling milk, then trying to push up from your chest or pick up a spoon becomes quite a workout, says Dr. Wurm. Infants must learn to do this in order to crawl. And they must crawl to strengthen their legs for walking. Just remember to prepare the area. You want to remove all potential choking hazards, including large objects with small, removable parts. Also, remember, sharp edges are bad. And you have to be able to see the kid. But you can resist the urge to disinfect or sanitize this space, says Dr. Wurm. Early exposure to the environment's microbes can help prevent allergies and autoimmune diseases later. "Dirt is good for babies," says Dr. Wurm.

Even cheaper than dirt—yet critical for our babies—is the favorable emotional bond called healthy attachment, says Dr. Wurm. There are no products sold in stores that promote healthy attachment, which is a beneficial psychological connection between a baby and his caretaker. This early feeling of security will continue to influence a child's social, emotional, and intellectual development throughout childhood.

Healthy attachment describes a baby's positive connection with her caretaker that develops because she knows that adult will attend to her needs. It's most important for us to respond between birth and six months. So if the baby cries, hold her. If the baby is hungry, feed her. If the baby has furiously pooped, wait until your fellow airline passengers are safely on the other side of a bathroom door. And then change her. The kid in turn develops true inner security, which leads to more independence and healthier relationships, says Dr. Wurm. All this holding and attention makes the kid believe the world is a safe place. She's then more likely to explore new situations, leading to greater cognitive and tacit development. Higher self esteem also helps build lasting and more trusting friendships. Because secure people are comfortable sharing their thoughts and feelings.

Don't worry if you're both working in jobs outside of your homes. Nannies, grandparents, and day care professionals are excellent at holding and feeding babies, says Dr. Wurm. And as parents, this is what we should be looking for when evaluating our caretakers. If a baby under a year old is happy to see her caretaker but shortly afterward goes back to the business at hand—finger-sucking, rattle-shaking, block-building, whatever's happening that moment—then that person is probably pretty good at attending to her needs. On the other hand, constant crying and clinging and the inability to separate all signal that something is wrong.

"We spend so much time as parents focusing on all the things a baby needs," says Dr. Wurm. "But all they really need is a loving adult in their lives who's meeting their needs in a very basic way." Oh, and they also need a stroller. The question is whether this stroller must charge your cell phone and become the designer item that establishes your high-ranking status among the new peer group called Other Mothers and Fathers.

My personal experiences: Most of the moms I knew—including me—had expensive models. While they were of varying brands, they did in a matter of weeks all become giant obstacles around which we had to navigate and squeeze past in garages and tight hallways. We used only our light umbrella strollers. They were nine pounds, a breeze to put in the trunk, and at around $39 were bargains we didn't mind buying. You can skip the entire $1,000 step!

In the meantime, choose a stroller with four wheels, a sun shade, and perhaps a cup holder—you may want to grab coffee or wine for this one—because walking your baby for even several minutes in both morning and evening is more than just lovely. It's an activity that supports your baby's circadian rhythm, says Dr. Wurm. That's the system that releases cortisol in the morning—the hormone keeping us alert and stimulated—and melatonin at night, which helps us sleep. The baby's brain will register the natural light as brightening or turning to dusk and will respond by releasing the appropriate hormone.

It's true, some of our babies will live through Miami summers or Maine winters. But aside from blizzards, hurricanes, or any other weather condition associated with flying debris, extreme climate shouldn't stop your stroller walks, says Dr. Wurm. Babies dressed appropriately—hats and blankets or gauze and linen—can be outside like anyone else.

The rewards come in several forms. Sleep cycles are important not only because you could use a full night's rest, but also because development is bountiful during these hours, seeing as the brain and the body finally have some time to themselves.

Not Buying It **Ever**

We're all for saving money, but never buy baby supplies, toys, books, trinkets, or—let's simply expand the category—*anything for your baby*—from a secondhand or thrift store. The prices might be tempting, but the product standards are subpar.

First, while it's illegal to sell any goods that have been recalled, many crib and child care items manufactured before new standards were created are not considered illegal.[25] Yet they still carry the same suffocation or strangulation hazards.

Second, it's completely legal for these stores to sell products with a higher allowable lead content. Lead poisoning can cause mental and neurological delays in kids, more so than in adults, because young nerves and brains are still developing.

Kids' bodies absorb lead when they put objects in their mouths. But they can also get lead poisoning by first touching a dusty or peeling lead object and then putting their fingers in their mouths or later eating food. Children also breathe in tiny amounts of lead.

Lead poisoning in children is typically cumulative, meaning, exposure can harm mental development over time, causing problems such as learning disabilities or speech delays, says Dr. Wurm.

Lead can also be instantly deadly. In 2006 a four-year-old girl died from swallowing a piece from a heart-shaped charm bracelet that came free with Reebok sneakers.[26] The jewelry—a seemingly innocent silver-colored chain link with a simple heart charm reading REEBOK—contained lethal levels of lead.

In 2007 and 2008, the Consumer Protection Committee found that manufacturers were exceeding the lead standards, which allowed for 600 ppm (parts per million).[27] It in turn issued stricter standards, lowering those allowable amounts to 100 ppm. Still—with the exception of children's metal jewelry—thrift stores and their counterparts were to be excluded from the rules when selling books, clothing, clothes, mirrors, metal furniture, and bicycles.

Rock-Solid Money Move

Forget the $1,000 stroller—there is only one purchase you can make that's proven to drastically improve your child's life: a college education. People with college degrees have higher incomes and less joblessness, according to the College Board.[28] They're more likely to have health insurance and are less likely to be obese. People with college diplomas more often volunteer in community organizations and less frequently smoke than those with only high school degrees. College graduates are more likely to vote.

What does this have to do with a stroller? You'll want to buy the cheaper one and invest the cash. Because raising a nonsmoker who works and votes is very, very expensive. By the fall of 2033, one year at a public, in-state university—tuition, fees, room and board—could cost $47,867, while one year at a public out-of-state school could cost $69,023, according to estimates calculated by Kalman A. Chany, author of *Paying for College Without Going Broke* and president of Campus Consultants, Inc. Private schools could cost $107,189 a year and an average Ivy League could cost $149,327. Putting aside $1,000 today would—if invested earning 7 percent interest—be worth $3,379 in eighteen years.

Estimated Cost of College Fall 2033–Spring 2034 (tuition, fees, room and board)

If tuition increases are . . .	4%	5%	6%
Tuition at a 4-year public in-state school will cost . . .	$39,909	$47,867	$57,314
Tuition at a 4-year public out-of-state school will cost . . .	$69,023	$82,786	$99,125
Tuition at a 4-year private school will cost . . .	$89,368	$107,189	$128,343
Tuition at a 4-year Ivy League school will cost	$125,699	$149,327	$177,106

(Source: Kalman A. Chany, author of *Paying for College Without Going Broke*)

If you're like most parents hearing those numbers for the first time, one of the following thoughts has likely entered your mind:

1. College tuition prices are too steep and would be best managed with denial. (Where did I leave my sunglasses, anyway?)
2. I'll incur those costs in eighteen years, which is precisely the amount of time I have allotted to writing a best-selling novel. That will be made into a movie.
3. My baby is incapable of waving hello, so this information doesn't apply to me.
4. My baby is waving hello before all the other babies and is therefore a genius destined for scholarships, so this information doesn't apply to me.

Those are all excellent points. Except to say there are no proven links between a person's toddlerhood waving and high school academic advancements. And even if—sorry, when, *when*—your novel sells, you'll still need to pay for college. If you have leftover money, you can simply use it to buy your yacht.

Many college savings plans won't hurt your child's chances for financial aid, and can even in some instances make it easier to get loans. It's more palatable for schools to help close the gap between the amount you've saved and the amount you need than it is to come up with the full tuition amount. Borrowing the entire cost of college is not great for your child either. Loans are expensive—at 8 percent interest, a $100,000 education winds up costing $145,593 if repaid in ten years—and delays other life events, such as starting a business, buying a home, and getting married.

So you see, a super-expensive nursery could pull our kids back from more quickly achieving world domination. Instead, we should each decide how much money to set aside each month using an online college savings calculator (there's one at ChooseToSave.org). And then direct those dollars into one of the following accounts.

SECTION 529 SAVINGS PLANS

Don't let the name bore you—Congress must have figured, "Why come up with pleasing names when you can just call things by their tax code?"—because these funds can have some exciting benefits. Putting your money into one of these plans is the same as buying a mutual fund that invests in stocks, bonds, or a combination. But if there are profits, you won't have to give the government its share of the taxes. That could be—assuming your investments appreciate—a lot of money. Capital gains are tax-free if—and only if—you use the money for college tuition, fees, or room and board. Think about it: If you're in the 25 percent tax bracket, then you likely give the government $150 for every $1,000 you earn in capital gains. But if that $1,000 is earned in a 529 plan and is used to pay for college, you can skip the entire part about paying taxes.

It's important to remember, however, that *investing* and *earning* are not interchangeable words. Yes, the S&P 500 tends to increase over time, but there's always the possibility that you'll be cashing out in the midst of a downturn. Your college savings are at the mercy of the markets. And in a less-than-shocking revelation, your investment managers also get to make money here. The funds and their managers will charge enrollment fees, annual maintenance fees, and asset management fees. Occasionally, some are waived, if you happen to be a big shot with your broker. But these fees are important to calculate when considering a plan because they cut into earnings.

When you buy your plans through a broker, you'll be charged a "load." This is another word for "commission," so do not assume your financial advisor will try to lighten yours. Still, brokers are often helpful in evaluating plans. The market performance of each fund can vary, and you'll want to pick one with great returns. That can be complicated. Some of these funds maintain that investors are successful only with professional guidance and refuse to sell their shares directly to customers.

But the diligent and the determined most certainly can buy funds without help. The College Savings Plan Network, created by the National Association of State Treasurers, has a website with links. You can open an account in any state—you don't have to live there—but some states offer tax benefits for keeping your money at home. For example, Colorado will let its residents who invest in the plan deduct from their state taxable income the entire amount of the yearly contribution. So if you put $1,500 dollars in that 529 plan, you can reduce the amount of income on which you pay taxes by that same amount.

Aside from the tax jubilee, another great thing about this program is that your child must use this money for college. What else would the kid use it for? Well, bottle service at night clubs, for starters. Some savings accounts make it possible for your kid to use the bounty for whatever they like. Also, with these 529 savings plans, if the child doesn't go to college, you can redirect the money to another child. Be warned: If you take the money out early, you have to pay not only taxes but also a 10 percent penalty.

529 PREPAID TUITION PLANS

Again, no one got more creative than the tax code in naming these, but 529 tuition plans let you lock in college for tomorrow (eighteen years' worth of tomorrows) at today's rates. You buy units or credits or years of college today (read: today's prices) at in-state schools. And you can cash these in when your kid enrolls. It's a pretty good deal considering college tuition and fees are projected to rise by between 5 percent and 7 percent, according to the estimates from Campus Consultants. It works well also for the school, which invests your money and hopes to keep those returns in line with its own tuition hikes.

Unlike the stock market investments of 529 savings plans, these are guaranteed by the state. Your child doesn't even have to go to the school through which you bought the program because the value can be transferred to out-of-state schools or even private schools.

Don't expect it to cover the full cost of private, however. If you're dead set on a private university, consider the prepaid tuition programs through the Private College 529 Plan. Like its state-sponsored sister program, we can lock in college for our young kids at today's rates, but because tuition costs more than state schools, these plans will also. Take a look at the schools participating in the plan; there are some 280 colleges and universities, such as Johns Hopkins University, Oberlin College, and Wake Forest University.

These plans are also guaranteed in that no matter what happens, participating schools would still accept the prepaid tuition for thirty years following your purchase, says Nancy Farmer, president of the plan. Private College 529 Plan members are the only colleges and universities who must accept those funds, but if your child chooses an outside school, you'll get back your contributions plus the market earnings or losses, but capped at 2 percent. Oh, also, the plans had to promise, when getting congressional approval, that buying into this plan wouldn't help anyone in the admissions process.

UGMA (UNIFORM GIFT TO MINORS ACCOUNTS)

These are accounts we can open in our kids' names. The child won't pay taxes because it's considered a gift, but if you give more than $14,000, you'll have to start writing that down because you're allowed to give $5.34 million without paying taxes throughout your lifetime. So clearly, you'll want to be careful with that.

You can open these accounts through a bank or brokerage firm. If you choose the latter, you can put stocks and bonds in them.

So because UGMA accounts are in the kid's name, one of three potential panic-inducing problems could occur. First, because the kid is the account holder, this money will count against anyone applying for financial aid. Second, when this child turns eighteen years old, he or she can use it to buy motorcycles or whatever seems like a good idea to an eighteen-year-old. And finally, this is the no-backsies of financial planning. This transfer is an irrevocable gift and you can't take it back. Yet, it's still a good option for those of us who need flexibility. You're not tied to the investments of the 529 savings plans, nor are you tied to a particular set of colleges. And if our kids don't go to college? They can use this money to fund an Internet startup.

TAXABLE ACCOUNTS

Hey, if you're an investment wiz, then to hell with all those special accounts and their fancy tax benefits. You can put aside as much money as you like, invest it, and use it to pay for college.

If the government isn't giving you special tax treatment, then it doesn't care *what* you do. (Well, it cares, but if you just had a baby, you won't have time to mastermind anything illegal.) You can however withdraw some for the kids' bat mitzvah or *quinceañera*. It's in your name, too, so even after the kid turns eighteen, you'll still have control. Savor this notion, as when the kid becomes a teen, your control is limited to very few departments.

CHAPTER TWO

Early Learning

choose

ACADEMIC ACCELERATION & FINANCIAL PROTECTION

OVER ADVERTISING HYPE

Save Estimated $5,107

The Stuff You'll Skip

Baby Literacy DVD volumes 1–5: $149.95

Baby Learning,
   Preschool and Childcare Complete Program: $491.39

A Learning Cube: $189.99

An Explorer Pad: $79.00

An edition of mind-building product: $18.95

Logic game: $8.95

Flash cards: $15.00

A combination of science and math learning tools:
$104.94

Music blocks $79.00

Play piano: $160.00

Mandarin Chinese Complete Set: $124.99

Total Cash Outlay: $ 1,487.15
Total Invested Savings after 18 Years: $5,026.47

Your baby *can* read, Dr. Robert Titzer assured parents. For more than fifteen years in national commercials touting his Infant Learning Company's products of the very same title—*Your Baby Can Read!*—he promised his products would give kids the edge they needed to succeed in life.[1] In testimonials, a mother identified as Kendra said, "If you do this program . . . your child will be thanking you when they are thirty years old and they have accomplished so much in life and they are brilliant people. You cannot put a dollar value on what you get back." (You can of course put a dollar value on the program, which had cost $200.)

The company used video graphics in cable and broadcast television advertisements to illustrate a growing brain, and Dr. Titzer said that when children develop reading skills during their natural window of opportunity—from about birth to age four—they read better and are more likely to enjoy it. Dr. Titzer's advertisements mentioned a "scientific study" and told us we had a short window of opportunity to start using the sliding word cards and lift-a-flap books that encompassed the Your Baby Can Read! program.

There was one teensy problem: Babies cannot read.

The Campaign for a Commercial-Free Childhood filed a complaint against Dr. Titzer's promises, gathering a slew of experts who agreed—in the words of Maryanne Wolf, director for the Center for Reading and Language Research at Tufts University—that the company's claims were "an extraordinary manipulation of facts." No one could find any scientific studies suggesting the children who learned to read before age five do better later on. NBC reporter Jeff Rossen could find only customer satisfaction surveys conducted by Titzer's company and some general studies that the doctors working with the CCFC said were "taken out of context." Nonie Lesaux, a human development professor from Harvard, and Dr. Karen Hopkins from NYU's Department of Pediatrics both said that the babies in Titzer's commercials were not reading and had at best memorized some words. Dr. Hopkins added that there is no evidence memorizing images of words can make you a better reader.

Even if baby word memorization were a desirable outcome, the American Academy of Pediatrics wouldn't likely recommend the route this program provided in getting there. Your Baby Can Read!'s viewing instructions would have our babies spend more than two hundred hours of screen time before the age of nine months. The AAP recommends babies spend a total of zero hours watching screens until they turn age two, linking the activity to sleep disturbances and delayed language acquisition as well as problems later in childhood.

In 2012 the government filed false advertising claims against Dr. Titzer and his company. Two years later, a settlement imposed a $185 million judgment (suspended after a $300,000 payment) on Dr. Titzer and barred him from using the phrase *Your Baby Can Read* with his products.[2] Dr. Titzer took what might be the only expected next step. He changed the product's name to Your Baby Can Learn!, which is a five-DVD set. Because while the law can impose severe financial penalties for deceptive advertising, the doctors at the AAP—who warn against screen time—can only dispense proven guidelines for healthy childhood development. And no one is forced to follow those.

Dr. Titzer is not alone. Companies like his are everywhere, selling us the idea that if our babies learn facts now, they will achieve greater academic success later. They have the answers in their products, from apps and tablets to elaborate toys—all backed by trusted research, of course.

No one can argue with the idea of early—and we mean *early*—childhood education. Kids who start out ahead in school very often stay ahead in school. Strong math and language skills at the start of pre-k and kindergarten are the educational foundations students build on in all subjects. It's true: Early education can lead to a lifetime of success, academically and beyond.

Thing is, the creator of all human life (God, apes, space dust, Simon Cowell, *whatever we each believe*) wanted to make things really easy and inexpensive on parents. So babies were—still are—born with brains that are built to most effectively develop through exposure to concepts that are simple, pure, and not purchased in stores: Math comes from pulling apart flower petals, and verbal skills are acquired by speaking with parents. On the other hand, hooking this delicate, soft cranial tissue up to electronic screens or blinking lights or even complex worksheets will surely short-circuit the wiring. It's not healthy. And it's not cheap.

But we fall for it. We're vulnerable—bombarded with terrifying facts while being soothed with heavy doses of fiction. First, we're told that the college admissions process has gotten cutthroat competitive. We all read *The New York Times* article reporting that Stanford University, for the class of 2018, got 42,167 applications and accepted just 2,138 students.[3] "Parents have been duped into believing that if they buy a particular toy or a particular so-called educational app, their children will have an educational advantage," says Kathy Hirsh-Pasek, a psychology professor at Temple University and author of *Escaping the Learning Illusion*. "We figure we'll do our best to accelerate their developments. And we have this real sense we can beef up their reading and math skills. We suffer from what we call 'The Learning Illusion.'"

And we forget the simple truth that American marketing executives are geniuses. They take universally accepted research saying, for example, kids most easily learn foreign languages before age seven, or babies learn best from play, and incorporate the findings on their product packaging. But because they're printed there does not always mean the product features correspond with the intentions of those scientific findings. Some of the products may have the opposite effects. Many of them—typically the most expensive toys—teach instant gratification rather than persistence and grit. Some are downright harmful to development, while others won't necessarily delay babies but have pricey paybacks that are debatable, at best.

Unfortunately, no one is governing the educational toy industry. Anyone can stamp the word *educational* on the box, and any expert might just support that label. But that's only because boxes themselves are quite educational, say pediatricians and researchers. Never mind the toy! You can cut up the box and build play spaceships.

That's the kind of hands-on learning through play that experts want to see. Creative story lines from spaceship building, engineering lessons from building a wooden block tower. Babies and toddlers need to develop a natural curiosity, to learn how to learn, and to socialize and cooperate. Not to stare at lessons created by Dr. Titzer. The important learning during your child's early years can best be achieved without much of what's for sale on the market.

The Setbacks of Screen Time

The American Academy of Pediatrics has issued warning after warning after warning—delivered several times in this book alone—about electronics and screen toys.[4] The brains of babies who have been crawling this earth for less than twenty-four months are incapable of putting academic concepts into the appropriate contexts, says Dr. Ari Brown, the lead author of the policy statement on media for the AAP. Kids this age gain knowledge through their five senses: sight, sound, taste, smell, and touch. Videos are passive experiences that kids can only watch from the sidelines of their bouncy seats. And while they may be entertained by the music or colors or dancing animals, they cannot touch, smell, or taste anything in the show. So exposure to math or reading using an app will not advance them intellectually or academically.

What's worse, the apps will delay language development. When a screen is on—even if it's a news station providing background noise—talking between babies and adults declines by 85 percent, says Dr. Brown. And speaking with our babies is the best way to propel their verbal abilities.

For all those reasons, if you ever want to incite a mad fury among of group of child development specialists, you can simply mention one of two products, both intended to park screens in front of babies' faces. The first is a potty with an "Activity Seat for iPad." This makes it possible for us to let babies watch cartoons while they're playing or peeing. It's a furniture concept that totally helps families avoid the constant aggravation of leaving electronics *in the other room* when their children are facing that pesky and familiar urge to eliminate bodily waste. Then there's the Fisher-Price iPad Apptivity Seat, which has been discontinued—the CCFC had been working on that—but had looked just like a bouncy chair with one added feature: an arm that reached above the seat to park in front of the babies' tiny faces a computer screen. Costs for both hovered around $50.

Most of the experts discussing these products with me couldn't immediately find the words to describe them, refusing outright to acknowledge them as toys. They're also pretty amazed at the idea of distracting kids during the very waking moments that are truly educational with a device that's known to hinder intellectual development. Because while kids subjected to these products might be kept quiet, it's probably not worth sacrificing the live and in-person action. To an infant-age audience, sandwich-making or a lip gloss application is considered an engaging performance. They learn stuff—even watching the gloss applicator return to its tube is physics.

The Campaign for a Commercial-Free Childhood (and its team of experts from institutions such as Columbia University and Harvard Medical School), in a complaint to the Federal Trade Commission regarding the Fisher-Price Laugh & Learn apps, reminded the government that most current research on child development and learning suggests that screen interactivity alone does *not* have educational value for young babies.[5] "There is significant risk," wrote Dr. Joshua

Sparrow, associate clinical professor of psychiatry at Harvard Medical School, "that parents who are naturally anxious to do everything in their power to maximize their children's potential and raise them to be successful adults in a highly competitive global marketplace—will err on the side of exposing their infants and toddlers to products claiming to accomplish these and related goals."

The government did not see it that way. The FTC said Fisher-Price wasn't making any specific claims.[6] The company didn't say, for example, that the apps improve literacy or school performance. The company didn't promise parents their kids would learn anything. Only that their product "teaches letters A–Z." And that's exactly what it does. Case closed.

Electronic toys are also heavy on instant gratification. When a child presses a button and a computer screen or light-up ball answers immediately with great electronic fanfare, babies learn to expect quick and instant results. But diligence and grit come from patience and hard work at a variety of tasks, says Dr. Wurm. Social skills and cooperation come from playing games with other children, not electronic voices. And learning to temper your mother's high-volume rages about not being a maid comes from cleaning up a giant mess. Not turning off a switch.

We may still find ourselves browsing a toy selection and drawn to a battery-operated sensation of lights and sounds. But despite their seemingly exciting offerings, those battery-operated or electronic toys could turn out to be less educational. "Old-fashioned retro toys," says Hirsh-Pasek, "such as red rubber balls, simple building blocks, clay, and crayons—that don't cost so much and are usually hidden in the back shelves—are usually much healthier for children than the electronic educational toys that have fancier boxes and cost $89.99." Here's why: When a toy can respond to a child, parents tend to assume their role in the matter is covered, says Hirsh-Pasek. She and her colleagues observed kids playing with traditional shapes sorters and also battery-operated models that "talk" to the child. And they discovered that not only do parents interact less with the child when the toy can respond, but also they less frequently use the spatial words—*over, under, through, far, between*—that help kids do better in a variety of math skills later.

Brain-Building: The New Reality

Years ago, University of Zurich researchers told us that if our kids learned to play instruments, their brains would grow.[7] Fair enough. They found that the cerebral portions controlling motor skills, hearing, the storage of audio information, and memory would magnify and become more active when a person learns how to play an instrument. A child's IQ, they said, can improve to the tune of seven points.

Heck, those of us without degrees in neurophysiology can accept quite easily that learning notes and their various fractions, determining their locations on a keyboard, or producing them with strings, and then afterward mastering the ability to simultaneously *read* while sending messages to the fingers to *play* those notes, can—of course—be healthy mental exercise.

But *that's* what the scientists mean in saying our kids should "play" classical music. They didn't mean we should teach them to press a "play" button and sit there eating crackers. Disney, with its Baby Einstein videos that played classical music from Ludwig van Beethoven and Johann Bach during baby-friendly puppet shows, made billions of dollars based on research and, afterward, made the most famous apology. After the government agreed that screen time was not an effective way to teach babies under two years old, Disney removed the word *educational* from their advertisement. Two years later the company, which bought the brand from its founder Julie Aigner-Clark in 2001, refunded the $15.99 for up to four videos per household for those who bought them between June 5, 2004, and September 5, 2009.[8] Before then, it had by some estimates been selling $200 million worth of the videos annually.

To this day, however, the surname of Albert Einstein—the German-born physicist who put forth the theory of relativity—adorns a litany of plastic toys. A few of them pertain to classical music, while many other toys' connection to Einstein is far less clear. And while no one is going to discount the value of music—it can help emotions to surface, for example, says Hirsh-Pasek—and there's rhythm and beat (which is mathematical), it won't likely do any brain-building or turn your child into a genius.

Ah, yes, brain-building. Parents don't expect toys to include in the packaging scientific proof—hell, we can barely figure out the assembly instructions. That's why it's been possible for some sellers to bypass research and instead rely exclusively on myth. Between 2012 and 2013 a company called Focus Education made about $4.5 million on its *Jungle Rangers* computer game—selling for $214 each—by telling parents it had "scientifically proven memory and attention brain training exercises, designed to improve focus, concentration and memory."[9] The company said its product could give children "the ability to focus, complete school work, homework, and to stay on task." The federal government said, essentially (and these are my words), "Yeah right: Where's your proof?"

Then there was the Brainy Baby Right Brain series, which would imply that the product was tailored to target the brain region responsible for creativity. And a handful of websites selling educational toys have adopted URLs with the *right brain* phrasing, as have a ton of product descriptions. Roger Sperry, who won the Nobel Prize in 1981 for his work studying epilepsy, developed the right brain–left brain theories. Modern neuroscience tells a different and more complicated story of the way parts of the brain work, says Hirsh-Pasek. For starters, impulse control comes from the frontal lobe. As for an analytical or creative side? In the most gifted math students, both the right and left brains were found to work together, according to research from US Army Research Institute for the Behavioral and Social Sciences.[10]

You may not be on the email distribution list of brain researchers, but you've probably still seen the headlines screaming that second languages and new accents are most easily acquired before age seven. Few factors are more effective in causing parents to respond with great urgency than those offering an age cutoff and a window of opportunity. Some parents—okay fine, me—have even bought one "toy" that, at the press of a button, recites the unique sounds of each language, such as the rolling *R* in Spanish, the twirling *oui* of French, and some forty other dialects.

It was a waste. Even if the window to learn languages is real—some research says it's not—buying books and tapes and toys for your children won't likely help much, says Heather Bortfeld of UConn. Learning a language is one of those proficiencies that a person—particularly a person of age four—develops because they must communicate information. People learn how to express themselves because it serves a purpose.

Very few toddlers are going to view the ever-changing global marketplace as a good reason to learn Portuguese. But if the grandparent in charge of the cookies refuses to distribute snacks in English, you can bet this kid will learn a few helpful, chocolate chip–related phrases. If the neighborhood friend who's usually available to play likes to speak in Spanish, then the language is likely to be contagious. On the other hand, pressing a button and hearing sounds or short phrases or studying flash cards and workbooks is a task of memorization that won't likely stick if the work is isolated to work. If our kids aren't using the phrases to communicate, they won't likely be reinforced. And your efforts have contributed only to the language that executives love: profits.

Then there are the extra academics after school. Kumon, at least if you're looking at revenues, appears to be a particularly popular program. By March 2009, the company had sales of $758 million[11] and more than seventy-five hundred Kumon centers in forty-eight countries.[12] Kumon will enroll your preschoolers as early as age two, in addition to your middle and high school kids. It costs about $200 a month and is a worksheet-based program Toru Kumon developed in 1954 in Osaka, Japan, because his son was having problems in math. Kumon has levels for preschool, which involve counting to 10, then to 120, and adding, as well as elementary and middle school levels. Success is based on speed and accuracy.

But the educators and pediatricians I spoke to have several problems with these programs, particularly for young kids. The first is that while yes, many students go on to secure great accolades, the company-selected testimonials don't prove that these kids—who are being raised by parents dedicated enough to education they're shelling out $200 a month for Kumon classes—wouldn't otherwise excel, says Dr. Wurm. She, for her part, doesn't disagree that early learning leads to great academic success. But she wants to see the studies proving that the kids in Kumon do better than the kids who read at home for thirty minutes each day. She wonders whether a child who tucks her head into a book filled with interesting material rather than worksheets won't more quickly develop a lifelong love for reading. Why are these expensive methods, which require transportation and appointment hours, better for developing early math skills than baking a cake and counting the eggs, looking at flowers and counting the petals, beading a necklace, or playing with marbles? She argues that concepts register quite effectively when parents simply put aside time for constructive fun.

At preschool ages and beyond, says Hirsh-Pasek, we need to teach our children the skills they'll need to be prepared for jobs in industries that have not yet been invented. To be successful, they'll need to be motivated to uncover new strategies and take risks. Self-starting, risk-taking, people-leading *visionaries*? Lofty goals, indeed. But we must prepare ourselves, parents, because the experts' next notion is the most astonishing of all: Getting our kids there is not expensive.

Raise Them Better for Less
CHILD'S PLAY

Dr. Kenneth Ginsburg, a pediatrician specializing in adolescent medicine at the Children's Hospital of Philadelphia and a professor of pediatrics at the University of Pennsylvania School of Medicine, went before a congressional subcommittee on behalf of the American Academy of Pediatrics and defended our children's right to play.[13] We—their very own parents—are taking away from them not only an activity that's really fun but also one that makes them smarter. I'm talking about play. We're not letting our kids play.

What the heck? Well, Dr. Ginsburg lists in his testimony a few perhaps familiar reasons we don't let our kids run around in the yard or sit in their rooms with dolls. We simply want to make the most of their time. It's not entirely our fault because, Ginsburg concedes, it's the message we're getting from every direction: Good parents actively build every skill and aptitude their child might need from earliest ages. And we dare not slow down the pace, lest our child be left behind. Play, from this perspective, seems a waste of time. So we focus instead on making sure our kids are building the resumes that will get them into good colleges.

Now might be a good time to mention that Dr. Ginsburg—at least from the looks of his webpage—appears to *also* be the kind of guy who cares about getting in to a good college. He holds two degrees in child and human development from the University of Pennsylvania and a doctorate of medicine from the Albert Einstein College of Medicine. In his testimony Ginsburg points out that unstructured play for our kids—letting them create the activity and the rules—is essential to their cognitive advancements and brain development. It enhances their learning readiness, learning behaviors, and their problem-solving skills; it burns calories and is intellectually enriching.

Play, explains Hirsh-Pasek, encompasses a few important C's necessary for learning content: collaboration, communication, critical thinking, creative innovation, and confidence. Building a sand castle or a living room fort involves a group's input as well as physics (certain angles will support the structure; others will cause it to collapse), not to mention creativity, as guest inhabitants could be giants, tiny aliens, jungle animals. There's no cost to failing. Instead, it's fun when a mountain of pillows comes crashing down and you have to start again. Or make up an entirely new game. This is the kind of process that develops confidence.

Playtime is more effective when it includes friends. Socializing has been found to improve the brain's executive function, which is responsible for working memory, self-monitoring, and the ability to suppress external and internal distractions, according to research from the University of Michigan Institute for Social Research.[14] There, scientists watched more than 192 adults and saw that pleasant conversations with other people boosted performance in an array of common cognitive tasks. "These findings highlight the connection between social intelligence and general intelligence," says Oscar Ybarra, the study's lead researcher.

As if you needed another reason to step away from the flash cards, kids who play with big wooden blocks and flimsy cardboard puzzles will effectively develop science, technology, engineering, and math skills. Those are disciplines commonly shortened to the acronym STEM. In the event you haven't been researching how your toddler will competitively navigate the high-tech job market, producing a population with these proficiencies is an organizational goal everywhere from the nation's school systems to national security. Blocks and puzzles provide an early foundation for the kind of higher test scores that can lead to an increased course load in these subjects and a better chance of a career in these high-paying fields. Essentially, researchers from our nation's top universities have proven it takes a $16.99 investment—the cost of a seventy-five-piece block set—to raise cutting-edge kids.

Don't believe me. Hirsh-Pasek and her colleagues found that kids who frequently played with blocks could also better perform on tests that assessed counting, measurement, and judgment.[15] In testing more than one hundred three-year-olds from various socioeconomic backgrounds, she found that those who could best copy block structures provided by researchers also had the highest scores in math skills ranging from simple counting to complex operations such as adding and subtracting.

It's not just that kids who are good at blocks are also good at math. The researchers controlled for IQ, testing them at the beginning and measuring improvements at the end. It's because a lot of reasoning goes into the construction of block architecture, including alignment, perception, spacing, weight distribution, and memory.

Meanwhile, researchers at the University of Chicago found a link between playing with puzzles and spatial skills, which is a unique type of intelligence that involves the ability to mentally visualize the rotation of two-dimensional and three-dimensional figures.[16] Kids who have strong spatial skills are more likely to take STEM courses at later ages and pursue careers in those fields as adults.

BOOK WORMS

When it comes to better reading skills, you don't need a $200 DVD series; you need a free library card. Even if our babies *could* read—and perhaps some of our toddlers can—they won't be mentally devouring the kind of material that imparts great wisdom or teaches an important lesson. The complexity of a toddler's book plot will be limited to Dick, Jane, and perhaps a few of their pets. The vocabulary will be basic, and balls and dogs can only be so exciting, says Dr. Wurm.

In order for our babies to be submerged in all that literacy has to offer, we must read to them. That way, we will be working with material that can impart new concepts and valuable lessons that can further fuel their verbal and social developments. The books we're capable of reading aloud to our kids will offer exciting story lines and narratives that include a beginning, a middle, and an end. Those pages can include moral lessons, character reactions both appropriate and inappropriate, and therefore subject matter for conversations between you and your toddler.

Toddlers love to ask "why?" and have been known to respond to even the most carefully thought-out articulations with another "why?" It's time to turn the tables. When it's possible, we should ask children to come up with the explanations. At University of Texas at Austin, researchers presented 182 children ages three to six with these cool mechanical toys that had colorful, interlocking gears with cranks on one end and propellers on the other.[17] Those who were asked to explain the mechanics outperformed those who weren't when it came to understanding the operations of the toy, rebuilding the toy, and transferring that new knowledge to other tasks. This forces them to think like scientists, according to researchers. They wind up not only better learning material, but also more able to connect the novel ideas with the concepts they already know.

Rock-Solid Money Move

Buying insurance is not fun, seeing as you get your money's worth only if you're disabled, dead, or being sued. And we certainly don't want any of those things to happen. But it's even worse if they happen without us having insurance. Insurance can shield our kids from — no exaggeration—homelessness and complete destitution. Seriously, if the high-income worker becomes disabled, then who will pay the mortgage? Even with a stretch, your family still needs food, gas, and electricity. If you have children, insurance policies are critical safeguards for the future: They'll protect our families if we can't.

Few people are going to be happier to hear from you than an insurance agent or broker. These people work sometimes entirely on commission. Because this business is based largely on referrals, they're often motivated professionals who work to provide personalized, quality products and hands-on customer service.

Unless they're thieves. The business model for insurance, in its purest sense, involves us making regular payments for a service we don't even *want* to use. It could be years before we even try! In the most common type of insurance fraud, according to the FBI, the agent pockets your premiums without sending them to the underwriter.[18] Rest assured, that underwriter has no record of you or your family when you go to file a claim.

That's why you cannot let yourself be intimidated by someone selling you insurance. If a particular policy sounds confusing, work only with a broker happy to explain it over and over again. You are not an idiot. On the contrary, if something sounds too complicated or too good to be true, it's possible that you've detected a red flag. Or at the very least, you've discovered you're working with a broker unwilling to work for those high commissions. If the situation feels heated or pressure-packed, find another agent.

You'll need to research your agent *and* the underwriter. If the company goes out of business, it's totally not paying your claims. States have entire commissions dedicated to monitoring the insurance industry; find yours at the National Association of Insurance Commissioners (www.naic.org). NAIC also has a database that will tell you if the agent has been disciplined in the past. And to research the financial strength of the company, head to the rating agencies, such as A.M. Best, Moody's, Standard & Poor's, and Fitch.

DISABILITY INSURANCE

Disability insurance covers a portion of your paycheck in the event you get hurt and can't work. Most Americans underestimate their chances of becoming disabled, according to the Council for Disability Awareness, which works to publicize some pretty depressing statistics. For example, the typical thirty-five-year-old woman standing five feet four and weighing 125 pounds, who doesn't smoke, leads a healthy lifestyle, and works mostly in an office, has a 24 percent chance of becoming disabled for three months or longer.

A typical male that age who is five feet ten and 170 pounds—with the same stats—has a 21 percent chance.[19]

In sharing more gloom, disability insurance is expensive. But that should only prove its great importance. Insurance companies make bets, and if they weren't so likely to lose this one, the policies would be a lot cheaper. Your premiums (the amount you pay for the policy, either monthly or in a lump sum) are affected by factors such as weight, age, occupation, and income. The typical cost is 1 to 3 percent of your salary. And while of course you should shop around, you have to be careful not to go by the lowest cost only. You'll want to enter this transaction armed and ready. That means knowing what your employer brings to the table, so have a talk with your benefits officer. Ask about sick leave or short-term disability. Your company might just cover costs for a month, and premiums will be lower if you don't need a policy to kick in immediately. Also, some employers offer to pay for a portion of your premiums. As in most situations involving free money, you're advised to take it.

Even so, it may not be enough. Group plans (those offered by employers) typically cover only 60 percent of your salary. While most experts suggest that's an appropriate ration, these payouts won't include bonuses and commissions. In order to figure out how much insurance you need, you must first figure out how much money it costs you to live. If your policy covers 60 percent of your salary, and you can live on that, terrific. In fact, if you can live on even less, you can spend less on premiums.

You'll want a policy that protects against accidents *and* illnesses. But the majority of disabilities come from medical problems, which, according to the Council for Disability Awareness, contributed to 62 percent of all personal bankruptcies filed in the United States in 2007 and half of all foreclosure filings in 2006.

Remember not to disregard anything as simply insurance lingo, because tiny, innocent-seeming letters can change everything. The difference between "own-occ" and "any-occ" is not a *tom-a-to/tom-ah-to* kind of thing, in that you won't be offered the same sauce, regardless of the one you pick. "Own-occ" is what most experts recommend we buy. Those policies cover us if we can't do our own jobs—the ones we had before becoming disabled. The "any-occ" policies kick in only if we can't do any of the jobs that require our education and training. They could have us sending out resumes at some pretty inconvenient times. If your policy has portability, it means you can take it with you if you leave your employer. That's a good thing.

LIFE INSURANCE

Life insurance is cheaper and that's good news for many reasons, but mostly because statistics prove we're actually unlikely to die early.

Chances of Dying From:
- Cataclysmic storm: 1 in 126,158
- A hornet, bee, or wasp: 1 in 71,107
- Legal execution: 1 in 79,815
- Air, space, and transport accidents: 1 in 7,229
- Cancer: 1 in 158
- Heart disease: 1 in 7

(Source: National Safety Council)

We need life insurance. It's essential for people like us who would—God forbid—leave behind spouses and kids who couldn't pay the bills if we were gone. In fact, staring straight in the face at those expenses is the first step to figuring out exactly how much life insurance you should buy. Look at your mortgage or rent, credit card balances, or car payments you'd want your family to cover. You may also want to make sure you leave enough for college tuition and the costs of your burial.

You may have some of that covered in your existing financial portfolio. Figure out the dollar value of the securities and balances of the bank accounts they'd inherit. Subtract that from the expenses they'll have and the debts they'll take over, and you know how much money you'll want the policy to be worth. Do not—I repeat, do not—buy more insurance than you can afford. If you stop paying your premiums, the company stops covering your family. Just like that! Any money already spent is gone and while sometimes you can reinstate the policies, you'd better not die in the interim.

Next you'll have to figure out what kind of policy to buy, and most experts will tell you it's an easy decision: term life insurance. It's the cheapest, most straightforward way to actually insure people. You buy a policy that lasts for a certain number of years—if your youngest is age three, then an eighteen-year policy is good, considering the kid will be able to support herself at age twenty-one. And when the policy expires, you stop paying and the company stops covering you. By the time your kid is twenty-one, you'll need much less insurance—perhaps for a spouse only—though at that time you'll be older and the rates will be higher.

There are three other types of life insurance that will cover you for life, and they also have an investment component. Many of them may appear tempting for the very reason that insurance is dreaded. Some plans let you borrow money from your policy and others move with the markets. They're usually more expensive and have a nice commission for your agent. But while investing in markets is typically an important part of your family's financial portfolio, there's no reason you can't do this separately with an investment advisor. And use insurance for the purpose of insuring people.

Whole life insurance has a death benefit but also a cash savings feature that allows your money to accumulate interest—tied to the company's long-run investments—over time. You can borrow money from your account, and if you die, it's deducted from the value your family gets. If you surrender (or give up) the policy, you get the cash back. They're often touted for their retirement benefits, but if you want to save for old age, traditional IRAs serve the same purpose with low commissions and favorable tax benefits.

Universal life insurance is similar. Your premium is placed into an investment fund managed by the insurance company. Each month, the costs of the term insurance policy and the administrative costs are deducted from your account, which rises at current market rates. They have a lot of flexibility, as you can tinker with premium payments or death benefits, adjusting them higher or lower. But one thing still holds: You're paying extra money for the insurance company to manage your money.

When you buy variable life insurance, the company puts your money into market assets. The amount that's left to your family if you die and the cash value are all based on the performance of the assets. This requires serious confidence in the market. If the market drops and you die, your family could get very little. This is more than an insurance policy, it's a security—as in stocks and bonds. And those are far from insured.

UMBRELLA POLICIES

These policies are great for people who have kids or dogs, seeing as both produce bountiful opportunities for unexpected lawsuits. Typically, if other kids get hurt in our homes or bitten by our dogs, their parents will sue. Homeowners insurance will cover the costs up to $100,000. But medical expenses could be much higher. That's where umbrella policies come in. They hover over both home and auto insurance policies and cover us from potential financially destructive legal storms.

If a high-earning exec slips in our homes and can't work for months, we could be responsible for her salary. It also covers you if your kids—they would never!—damage someone else's property. Or if our dogs cause some destruction of their own. What if you cause an auto accident—meaning it's your fault—that results in $500,000 in damages? Not to mention legal fees. Most car insurance policies cover up to $250,000. Your umbrella policy can kick in and cover you for the rest.

Umbrella policies are not particularly expensive; most of us can get $1 million in coverage a year for just $300 per year. And simply discussing with agents our vulnerabilities to unfortunate incidents can help to make us more aware. And more safe.

CHAPTER THREE

Your Home

choose
PERFECT TIMING
OVER THE TWO-HOUR COMMUTE

Save Estimated $800,000

The Stuff You'll Skip

Home equity represents a substantial portion of American wealth, but from January 2007 to December 2011, four million Americans lost their home to foreclosure, according to a report by University of Central Arkansas professor Pam Bennett.[1] And 48 percent of people estimated that the value of their home had dropped. The goal is to avoid paying more money for your home than it will be worth when you're trying to sell it.

Total savings: Your life savings

Just after announcing their pregnancy, my friends Larry and Gayle bought their dream McMansion in a suburb of Cleveland. Located in a township created by developers who'd freshly bulldozed farmland, they chose a municipality with a name that was dripping with affluence. Something to the tune of Meadow Woods Country Manor Estates. The home brought the great promise of happiness an American family can achieve only by acquiring an oversize kitchen, a sprawling master bath, and fifteen-foot ceilings. Larry happily embarked on his new two-hour commute to work, shrugging his shoulders and saying, "Oh, it's not bad," before reminding us about all the reading one can accomplish on a train ride.

That's hardly debatable—we all want more reading time. But what might be worth examining are the motives behind American families' lust for larger homes. Homes are the single most expensive aspect of raising kids, according to the government report *Expenditures on Children by Families*.[2] And newly constructed houses have, on average, increased in size by 53 percent since 1973, according to the Census Bureau.[3] Used to be only 23 percent of new homes had four or more bedrooms. In 2014, 46 percent of houses were built that way, while the ratio of houses with three or more stories has doubled. Unofficially, new homes are designed with features that provide for more space and greater privacy. While these features most certainly come in handy when they're newly acquired and we're touring our friends around, pointing out our capacity for wine storage—which again, is awesome—experts wonder where we got the idea that sprawling living rooms and child-centric wings are essential for successfully raising kids.

Big houses are not bad for families, not at all. But we seem to have collectively decided that when it comes to living quarters, bigger is better in every circumstance. That each of us needs space and privacy. That all our friends have a big house, so we should get one, too. Because the more square feet of living space a family has, the happier that family will be. These houses—we may have come to believe—are tangible measures of our happiness and success.

And that's 100 percent false.

The correct answer to the home-buying equation—location, price, size, features—will be unique to each of us. What we need to get out of our heads is that a high standard of living absolutely depends on brand-new bath fixtures and twelve-foot ceilings. Or that residing far from our jobs, extended families, or favorite sources of cultural entertainment are sacrifices we're making for our kids' sake.

Kids thrive in smaller houses, which by design can help them dodge some invisible struggles that later plague adolescents and teens. For starters, these homes create more convenient backdrops for family communications and cultivate bonding between siblings. Sometimes smaller homes are closer to a city and cut down parents' commutes. Rest assured, you will not find me advocating for parent-child cosleeping here. Only this question: Who was it to decide that each of our kids should have their own bedrooms? It most certainly was not a child development expert from an esteemed institution. And it definitely was not a pediatrician who uncovered any great benefits on this front. In fact, there's no research stating that children, particularly young ones, thrive more fully when they can close the door and be alone.

On the contrary, room-sharing has a litany of psychological benefits, starting with the sense of emotional protection at bedtime. Because the frontal lobe of a child's brain is still developing between the ages of two and five, kids cannot separate imaginary life from real life, says Dr. Wurm. That explains why the Tooth Fairy is believable, as is the excuse on one occasion (I fell asleep, sue me) that she is unavailable Tuesday nights. Nevertheless, this fusion of realities will also account for kids truly believing there are monsters in the closet.

And having a sibling in the room offers a security they might not be able to express or even realize. That presence can combat resistance to bedtime and can foster peaceful sleeping, says Dr. Wurm. That doesn't mean peace will remain through all waking hours. Small disagreements and full-scale wars, complete with the hurling of toy-car missiles, are a certainty among all siblings, including those who share a room. But even that clashing can set the stage for the kind of sibling connection that lasts a lifetime. First, they'll learn to negotiate. One wants to use the desk, the other wants the top bunk for a night, and then there's the issue of that third, spacious shelf in the closet. Soon a treaty is formed. The next step is collaboration, and unfortunately, we are likely to be the target opponents in this scenario. Room-sharing provides so many ways for sisters or brothers or even combinations— though there are benefits to separating those kids before puberty—to work together as a team. Perhaps they'll hide a mess, clean a mess, help out with homework, plan a party, play a game, sneak in snacks, and pretend to be asleep. A bunkmate provides kids with a built-in confidant, which is not available to kids who sleep privately. Just like us, kids regurgitate the day as their heads hit the pillow, says Dr. Wurm. So even though your severe threats involving sleep time have gone ignored, understand that this pillow talk offers an opportunity for bonding. A strong sibling bond has lifelong benefits, as siblings provide a positive and protective influence that can make life easier from adolescence to adulthood. Brothers and sisters are a kid's comrades who can share earliest memories, family friends, and also childhood issues, on which they will collectively blame us, their parents.

When they're not fighting over closet space, kids are often found watching television. That's why it's handy when your TV can be heard from around the house. It may not *feel* like a great thing—seeing as many of the shows for kids can provoke in adults the urge to smash the offending electronic device with a baseball bat. But the rewards come when we're able to effortlessly monitor what our kids are watching. We overhear what's happening on the screen while we're making dinner or checking our email. We can scream, "Change the channel," or simply step in and magically appear for a teachable moment, educating our kids on being careful consumers during commercials. While fast-food chains and toy makers are trying to hold them captive, we can explain that people on television may seem beautiful and happy stuffing fries in their mouths. But they are acting. We can explain that toy helicopters don't fly by themselves and that assembly is always required. These commercials aren't trying to help us. They're trying to sell us.

It's simple: The more opportunities a family has to communicate, the more a family will communicate. Smaller houses encourage the kind of unscripted moments during which real teaching and genuine communications occur, says Dr. Wurm. The best discussions aren't planned, she says, but are sparked from passing each other in hallways or from sitting around a kitchen island. Smaller homes give kids and adults easy access to each other, making the spontaneous expression of a thought or daily event practically effortless.

If the size of your house means kids are sick of seeing you all the time, good, tell them to go outside. Rather than lounging around on leather sofas, Dr. Wurm wants to see our kids spend time outdoors, particularly in green or wooded areas. This enhances their physical and mental well-being. Sunlight and trees are natural mood elevators, and exercise improves a kid's ability to learn and concentrate. Studies from the University of Illinois point out that kids score better on tests after exercise,[4] and separate research proves even children with ADHD display higher levels of focus after coming in from outside.[5] Playing in natural environments, says Dr. Wurm, has been found to temper ailments, including asthma and nearsightedness. And it offers the ability to promote a child's creativity, problem solving, and emotional and intellectual development. That's why in addition to focusing on square footage, we'll do well to consider a home's distance from our kids' schools. Typically, giant houses are located on big lots and surrounded by winding roads and sealed by gates. Smaller ones tend to be walking distance from schools. And kids who can walk or bike to school will have improved levels of concentration that last for over four hours.[6] A study from Dutch researchers found that third-grade kids who got a blood-pumping commute to class also saw their academic abilities increase to the equivalent of a child a half a year further in their studies, wrote researcher Niels Egelund, who coauthored the report. This effect did not occur in kids who were driven by parents or public transportation.

Your own commute time is also critical to consider. Big houses and backyards sound romantic, but experts warn that long daily treks to work can suck the life out of our marriages, our families, and our overall mental well-being. In a study of 208 commuters who took trains from New Jersey to Manhattan, environmental psychologists from Cornell and Polytechnic University tested each commuter's saliva for the stress hormone, cortisol, had each subject and his or her spouse answer a questionnaire,[7] and gave the commuters a simple task to perform after one particular trip. The conclusion: Commuting is stressful—even when we're just sitting there, riding trains. It also erodes our ability to carry out even simple undertakings. And life at home is packed with those, from checking homework to reading the kids a book before bed. Commuting can even cause divorce, if you believe one particular study from Sweden.[8] There, researchers concluded that long-distance commuters had a 40 percent higher risk of separating, and that even though many of the two million travelers in the study—mostly men—had advantages in terms of income and career opportunities, the first years of commuting were trying for their marriages.

"It's important to highlight the social consequences that commuting entails," wrote Erika Sandow of Umeå University. "For instance, how are children affected by growing up with one or both parents communing long distances to work?" If the answer is one parent is missing dinnertime, then the family will likely be lacking more than just a place setting at the table. Dozens of studies found that eating family meals together will benefit adolescents well beyond the dinner table, thanks to the routine, consistency, and socialization that those dinners provide.[9] Young people whose families regularly ate dinner together spent more time on homework and reading for pleasure. They had decreased reports of drug use, suicidal tendencies, substance abuse, and eating disorders.

This is not to say that people in big houses won't be home in time for dinner and will somehow neglect to communicate with their drug-addicted kids. Please. Besides, how could we even define the words *big houses*, seeing as it would have a far different definition for a family in New York City than it would for a Texan? Rather, the idea is to introduce some alternative considerations when contemplating the homes we choose and evaluating their locations and sizes. Or even during those unfortunate times when we compare our lives to other people's lives. It's true, many families—hopefully most—with colossal kitchens will do a great job of organizing meals and sibling-bonding opportunities. But considering the true developmental needs of our kids, those families without so much space will not be doing even one bit worse.

Raise Them Better for Less

Most of us shopping for a home will firstly have in mind the amount of money we want to spend, regardless of the size and location we ultimately select. That's because this is also an investment—a place to park our money and watch it grow—rather than purely a consumption purchase. Learning the economic indicators to navigate the real estate market is your Rock-Solid Money Move here. But in the meantime, there are some variable costs you could be able to cut.

1. ENERGY

Big houses use more electricity and they cost more to heat and cool. Newer homes, despite being larger, tend to have more efficient appliance systems. Still, homes with about 2,400 square feet spent $2,284 on energy each year, while homes with 4,000 square feet got electric bills of more than $3,430.[10]

That means even when considering two homes with the same price, the bigger one will ultimately cost an extra $1,100 a year—and that's a conservative estimate. It would grow more extreme during a particularly hot summer or cold winter.

If you choose an older home, you might buy your own energy-efficient appliances and electronics. The US Department of Energy stamps an Energy Star label on all sorts of stuff, indicating that—though up–front costs are higher—it will use less electricity or heat and offer long-run savings.[11] Consider: An Energy Star clothes dryer uses 20 percent less energy. If everyone in America had one, we'd collectively save $1.5 billion each year. Solar water heaters cut water bills in half, saving us $140 annually or about $2,900 over the life of the model. There's an Energy Star version of everything, from cordless phones to televisions, ceiling fans, and handheld vacuums.

2. CLEANING

The average American family of four spends about $906 a year on laundry and housekeeping supplies, a figure that grows with the size of your home. But the biggest cost here is not monetary, it's mental. The bigger the house, the more space there is to clean. Housecleaning is never finished. Rooms you don't even use get dusty. And even after believing you've made great strides, you're faced with the dilemma of tossing your yogurt container into a freshly emptied garbage bin or leaving it on a newly scrubbed countertop. You're constantly working against yourself. Not to mention your manicure.

3. PROPERTY TAXES

Property taxes can jump dramatically from one city to the next, even if they're adjacent. Typically, a municipality will tax you between 1 percent and 3 percent—sometimes up to 4.2 percent—of your home's value to use for roads, schools, police, and hospitals, whether you use them or not. Taxes for a $350,000 home could be $10,500 (with a 3 percent rate) in one location and $5,250 (with a 1.5 percent rate) a mile away. The difference of a mile could mean $5,250 each year.

4. MAINTENANCE

Homes are constructed with breakable parts: pipes, roofs, walls, floors, fireplaces, stairs, sinks, gutters, siding, and plumbing. These things frequently require repair or replacement and usually at the worst possible moments. That reminds me, emergency repairs are more expensive.

We're supposed to budget about 1 percent of our home's purchase price—keep it in an easy-to-access savings account—for repairs and maintenance, says Realtor.com. And that's fair; you'll use it all some years and won't touch it other years. Even certificates of occupancy don't guarantee everything is in perfect working order. Brand-spanking new homes may come with warranties, but once those expire you could be left owning a structure that's never been tested by a winter storm like the one brewing the week after you move in. Chinese drywall anyone? Ah, yes, that mold-breeding product was a newly constructed disaster.

5. ADDED AND UNEXPECTED INTEREST PAYMENTS

America might be the land of the free, but if you want to buy property, it costs a lot of money. Thankfully, it's also the home of the brave, meaning that if you are heroic enough to maintain good credit (and fearless enough for lawn care) you can likely find a bank to lend you the funds needed for home ownership. These loans are called mortgages and people don't actually distribute them or award them. They *sell* them. On commission.

When it comes to home loans, some of us will pay as much or more in interest—that's the price of the loan—than we will for the home itself. For example, if we were to borrow $300,000 at 5 percent interest over thirty years, we pay back not only the $300,000 but also $362,000 in interest, spending $662,000 for a house that costs $300,000.

That heart-pounding reality will prompt us to shop for low interest rates. Even if it didn't, the most credible economists would step in, declaring during low-rate periods that the time to buy is now. Lenders can latch on to those economic realities, twist them, create a little fine print, underline a few key words, and trick you into signing mortgages that are more costly than they seem.

Most of us have been warned and are well versed in the unpredictability of adjustable-rate mortgages (if not, *adjustable-rate* means your monthly payments can raise without warning). That's why shady lenders are tinkering with the way they sell fixed-rate loans, which denotes the rate over time won't change. But in response to our confidence in those products, they've created loans that stay fixed for an introductory period, sometimes only thirty days. And then—poof—they become adjustable and at the mercy of economic conditions that are far from fixed. Make sure you ask: Is the "fixed" interest rate there for the life of the loan?

Sometimes lenders say "very low rates." This can be sneaky if they're referring to the "payment" amount. The payment is the money going toward your equity (your ownership) in the home. You want that to be high. Your *interest* rate is the bank's profit. It helps only if that's low.

Questions to Ask while Mortgage-Shopping

We should shop around for mortgages, and the Federal Trade Commission has a checklist of questions to ask and a worksheet to help.[12] You can take this with you when you're shopping for a loan and speaking with officers.

Questions include:

- What's the down payment? When you're shopping for loans, don't focus only on the monthly payments. The amount you're required to have up-front is also pretty important. The higher the payment you make, the less you'll spend each month.

- Ask whether the rate is fixed or adjustable. If it's adjustable and interest rates rise, your mortgage rate goes up, and generally so do the monthly payments.

- Ask about the loan's APR (annual percentage rate.) You'll want to know the interest rate plus all the points (the fees you pay to the lender): broker fees, credit charges, and anything else you might be required to pay in a yearly rate. Ask for them to be quoted to you as a dollar amount, not just "points," so you know what you really have to pay.

- Ask about fees. A home loan often involves charges, such as loan origination or underwriting fees, broker fees, and settlement (or closing costs). Every lender or broker should be able to give you an estimate of its fees, and many of these fees are negotiable. In some cases, you can borrow the money needed to pay these fees, but doing so will increase your loan amount and total costs. "No cost" loans are sometimes available, but they usually involve higher rates.

Rock-Solid Money Move

Buying a home can be a very good investment. But only if we do so under three conditions:

1. Pay the right price
2. At the right time
3. In the right location

Perhaps you are old enough to remember the economy's recent and dire plummet into the real estate recession of 2008. No? Here's a short recap: Millions of people bought properties and later discovered they could no longer afford to pay for them. They also couldn't sell them. Markets sank in value. Millions of people were forced to give the properties back to the bank, losing the down payment and the mortgage payments. Let's try to prevent that from happening again.

There are many economic guidelines that hint to where the market is headed. They are actually called "economic indicators." Do not be intimidated by the idea of reading economic indicators. Think of them as you would chocolate-coated energy bars. Nobody can understand or pronounce *what* goes into these things. But everyone can compare the number of calories or fat grams in each one. Economic data is the same. Producing it is very difficult, requiring advanced degrees (and ugly clothes). But reading economic data is easy. You're simply comparing two numbers. Bigger or smaller. More or less. Growing or shrinking. The only skill to master here is a basic proficiency in the number sequence. Are you aware that 8 is greater than 7? Good. Can you determine whether the numbers 99, 100, 101 are *increasing* or *decreasing* in value? We can get started.

Afterward, you should be able to predict the real estate market with the same accuracy as any professional economist, meaning you will likely be wrong about *something*. Markets react unexpectedly to rate hikes, storms, national disasters, stock market gains, and international events. But you're also going to get a good sense of the economic climate you're entering. You'll be making your biggest financial investment with an eye on the market's direction, demand strength, affordability, and even your very personal price point, which you can determine for yourself, rather than relying on a realtor.

STEP 1: HOW TO MAKE SURE YOU PAY THE RIGHT PRICE FOR YOUR INCOME

Real estate brokers work on commission, meaning the more money you spend, the more money they make. Thanks to this mathematical fact, they have every interest in convincing you to buy a bigger, grander, more gorgeous home. Looking at properties you can't afford is either depressing (when you return to your range and find you cannot have French doors) or more likely, financially devastating. French doors have been known to negatively affect a person's judgment and cause overspending. It's best to enter your first meeting armed with your own price point.

Back in 2006, a spokesperson for the National Association of Realtors taught me an equation we can use to determine for ourselves a price point most suitable for our unique incomes. Perhaps because mortgage products have evolved, allowing us to buy more expensive homes with less income, the publicists there don't hand it out anymore. But I have held on to this tried-and-true equation because it's conservative. It's a guideline, but a very good one to keep you safe. If you want to effortlessly make mortgage payments, you shouldn't peek—and I mean do not even peek—at properties costing 40 to 50 percent more. If we follow its lead, this number will put us in control of our financial decision and keep us in safe funding territory. This method is the crisp white shirt or little black dress of real estate economics. This evergreen formula dictates:

1. Down payment worth 20 percent of the home's price
2. Thirty-year mortgage
3. 25 percent of our incomes spent on that mortgage

That last one, spending 25 percent of your income on your mortgage, means some of us will have to adjust the calculation. Maybe you send your children to private school or believe strongly in Italian sports cars. Anything that sucks up more of your money and leaves less for housing will alter the outcome of this equation. To accommodate for extreme expenses, alter the amount of your income you use for the equation by simply subtracting those amounts. For example, if you earn $100,000 a year and spend $50,000 on private school, consider your income for this equation to be the $50,000 you have left over.

Step one: Determine the affordability factor, and understand how to use it. You can calculate it yourself by looking at the Housing Affordability Index on the National Association of Realtors website (www.realtor.org/topics/housing-affordability-index). Or you can just take this number from www.TheHomeEconomist.com and skip the first math step. Whatever you do, remember that this number changes every month.

In the event you would rather do this yourself, you'll need to find the following numbers from the National Association of Realtors' Housing Affordability Index:

1. The nation's median home price (as of March 2015, $212,400)
2. The nation's median qualifying income ($47,000)

Divide the median price by the income (using today's numbers: $212,400/$47,000 = 4.5). That's called "The Affordability Factor."

We take that number—4.5—and multiply it by our own income to find the target price we should look to pay.

For example:

Mobile, Alabama:
financial manager ($75,430) and stay-at-home spouse

• Household income = $75,430

• Affordability Factor = 4.5

• Home Price = $339,435

• Down payment = $67,887

• Loan amount = $271,548

San Diego, California:
chemical engineer ($85,610)
and insurance underwriter ($64,610)

- Household income = $150,220
- Affordability Factor = 4.5
- Home Price = $675,990

- Down payment = $135,198
- Loan amount = $540,792

Now suppose the New House Idea wasn't entirely your idea. Say instead your real estate agent casually mentioned that a home similar to yours and down the street sold for $450,000. *What*, you're thinking. *I paid only $300,000!* If your house fetches a similar price, your family could perhaps buy a bigger house that would be more organized. (Seeing as a fraction of the profits would be spent at the Container Store.)

Here's how to calculate what you can afford when taking into account the profits from a home sale.

1. Multiply the Affordability Factor by your income.
2. Add the amount of profit from the sale of your home.

Once you understand the Affordability Factor, and what it means for your income, you're ready to start analyzing the other market conditions.

STEP 2: BUY OR SELL YOUR HOME AT THE RIGHT TIME
The Housing Affordability Index

People love to talk about real estate. They live in real estate. They buy it. They sell it. Their net worth depends on it. People really start to believe they could be real estate moguls. They stand around at cocktail parties and barbecues saying things like, *It's a good time to buy real estate*. And while "It's a great time" is excellent advice on whether to pay admission to a nightclub, you'll need more information when deciding whether to invest your life savings into the real estate market. Economists don't have crystal balls, but they do have access to economic indicators that show the market's strength and hint as to whether it's building muscle or taking a breather.

We Home Economists—a.k.a. mere mortal parents—can also figure out which direction the market is moving. The Housing Affordability Index from the National Association of Realtors will reveal whether a market is affordable or overheated. If we want to make (not lose) money on our homes, we have to pay a price that will turn out to be less than what we'll sell it for later. The whole buy-low-sell-high principle very much applies here. The Housing Affordability Index can help you determine the state of the national real estate market. (You can also pull this one out at cocktail parties when discussing real estate.) And while some local areas are protected from economic forces, most home prices are vulnerable to market conditions.

Generally, if you determine that real estate prices are affordable, it could be a very good time to buy a home. If the index indicates prices are expensive, you may want to wait. Prices might be rising, but the market's peak will come eventually. Let's be clear: *That's a bad time to buy*. It's called a "peak" because it doesn't get any higher. It drops off. On the contrary, the market topples over, bringing down home values to levels lower than what you've paid. Then, there's the opposite: No one wants to sell a home when all it will fetch is bottom-market prices. Remember that these are guidelines, and every situation will vary. (My husband, who is a lawyer, made me write that.)

The Housing Affordability Index is a number that tells us if the typical US homebuyer has the money for a typical US home. If the Typical Buyer has more than enough money to acquire a Typical Home, an economist—which in this scenario will be you—can assume that the housing market is affordable. If the Typical Buyer's income is in line with the average home price, economists assume the market is in line with itself, not too high and not too low. If the Typical Buyer does not have enough money too afford a median-priced home, economists—again, that's you—say the market is expensive, possibly overpriced. *Overpriced* does not have a different meaning in real estate than it does anywhere else.

You can read the index by inserting it into the following sentence: An index level of ____ means a person earning the median income has ____ percent of the money needed to buy a median-priced home. (For example: An index level of 140.9 means that a person earning the median income has 140.9 percent of the income needed to purchase a home.) You could decide from this that an average person has more than enough money to buy an average home. Or that the average person has enough money to buy an above-average home. That would make the real estate market affordable. If the housing affordability index is 97, it means that the average person has 97 percent of the money needed to buy the average home. Not enough. You can interpret this to mean that prices are very, very high. Prices move in the opposite direction of the index. When the index moves higher, home prices are becoming more affordable.

The index has proved, over the past twenty years, to be a good warning of high-priced real estate markets. I matched up the time series of indexes with famous real estate market highs and lows and found that during periods when it seemed everyone was getting richer and buying big expensive homes—and just before it all ended and real estate prices began to once again drop—the Housing Affordability Index had warned economists. (Again, in this scenario, the "economist" is you.) In the form of a single number—and particularly when we look at that number over several months—this index can tell us a lot about where the real estate market is headed.

Below there are guidelines to interpreting the numbers, using the stories they've told since the early 1990s. Just be sure to note, when you see that indexes of 110 tend to mean the market is very expensive, you will say, "Hey, if the Typical Buyer has 110 percent of the money she needs to buy a home, that's more than enough. Ten percent more, to be exact." But when I matched up numbers to dangerous drops in the real estate market, they have occurred as the index touched those levels. There are reasons for this. First, it's because this measure was created in the 1980s. And while leggings managed to make a comeback, the banking conditions of that time are gone forever. Today there are more mortgage products that help make home ownership more affordable. It's a financial move you can make with less money.

Second, the index's components consider only the down payment and the monthly payments. They don't consider closing costs and fees. Once a home buyer pays those, that buyer has less money. Just like going on vacation requires more money than airline fares and hotel rooms, buying a house requires more than down payments and monthly payments.

Another aspect to consider is not merely the index but the direction the index has been moving for six months prior. The housing market may be affordable, but if it's been falling, then it's likely becoming *more* affordable. This is something to consider if we're selling our homes. If we're getting offers that seem weak, but signs point to the market deteriorating, it could be a clue that we should take what's on the table.

Index of 110 and Lower

Buyers: Readings of 110 or lower signal that the real estate market is very expensive. It means the average person has 110 percent of the money needed to buy the average home. Sounds like the market's in line. But indexes registering this level have in the past signaled market problems. When home prices were at record highs in August of 2006, the Housing Affordability Index fell to 100.9. In 1989, another historically high-priced period, the index fell to 109.6 and stayed in that range until late 1991, when it shot up to 111. This suggests that indexes hovering around 100 indicate white-hot markets.

Sellers: Expect to get top dollar for your home, meaning if a good offer arrives, take it. Don't get overly greedy, because history proves these high prices will not last forever. Perhaps—*perhaps*—they'll get a little higher next month. But also there's a chance you'll kick yourself for missing this market. Speaking of profits, take yours to a financial advisor and consider parking them someplace other than property for now. If the market turns down, you'll be happy you decided to rent or bunk with your mother-in-law (yes, it's that serious).

Index of 120 to 130:

Buyers and Sellers: This is the most average of markets for everyone. Buyers should find fair prices and sellers should be able to pocket solid profits. The forces don't overly favor either party, so barring any below-the-belt dealings, no one has an unfair advantage.

Index over 140:

Buyers: If the past proves anything, now's the time to buy real estate. Home prices are ultra affordable and on average very low. The only question is whether they're going lower, and the next few entries will help you determine whether they will drop more. Check to see the market's direction by looking at the six months prior.

Sellers: Avoid selling in this market. If you can't afford your mortgage, try modifying your loan. If you want to downsize, you'll do it more successfully when the market rebounds. If all else fails and you still hang the For Sale sign, make sure you hire the toughest broker in town, one who can boast about a strong sales record. In a market with so few properties for sale, your listing is very important.

Months Supply

Whether you're buying a home, selling one, or just complaining about the process, you'll need to know who is in control: the buyer or the seller. But this isn't enough. It's like hearing on the news that it's warm outside. How warm? Warm enough to wear a tank top? To need sunscreen? To die of heatstroke? It's similar for the market. You need to know to what degree you could get burned. It's information that can give you great negotiating strength.

The favorability of market forces might affect your next move. If they're way out of favor, you might decide it's a bad time to make your move. If the forces are in your favor but the index indicates that could soon change, you might act quickly rather than hold out for a price that may not come for years. If you're the one with the power, you might ask for even more than a good deal on price. For example, home owners are supposed to leave window coverings—they're customized for those windows, anyway—and also lighting fixtures. But if it's a buyer's market, meaning there's an abundance of inventory and sellers are competing for your attention, you might ask them to throw in the rugs. If you're selling in a seller's market, when homes are scarce and prices are high, you may have other requests. Maybe you want to take your favorite chandelier. Or remain on the site an extra few months. Closing dates and conditions are also negotiable. The party in power may be able to orchestrate some convenient conditions.

To gauge whether it's a buyer's market or a seller's market, you'll see how long homes sit out there, unsold. This is found in a number called Months Supply, produced by the National Association of Realtors, telling us how many months' worth of homes are on the real estate market, and if you buy vodka you already understand. "Honey, we have a six-month supply of vodka in here." So, it would take six months to drink all the vodka in the house. But we're not measuring vodka, we're measuring homes for sale, so a Months Supply of 6 means it would take six months to sell all the homes on the market. As the month's supply piles up and depletes, the power shifts from buyers to sellers. When there are a lot of homes on the market, the buyers are in power. When there are very few and demand is high, the sellers are in power.

Here's how to approach real estate shopping while considering the Months Supply.

Months Supply of 7 to 8 or higher— Buyer's Market (Shoppers Hold the Power)

Months Supply of 7 to 8: When it would take seven to eight months to sell all the homes on the market, it's a buyer's market. But because this range is on the cusp, buyers are either beginning to get power or are about to lose it. You can decide which one by looking at the past twelve months.

If the numbers are getting bigger (for example, January was 6, February 6, March 7, April 8, etc.) a buyer's market may be underway. If that's the case, this is a fine time to shop but propsective buyers shouldn't feel any pressure to make a too-quick offer or suck up anything too unsavory, such as a questionable roof. Chances are, conditions for you are improving. Buyers are starting to gain power.

If you're selling, try to remember exactly that—buyers are gaining power. The environment for you isn't overly difficult yet, but if the trend continues, your home could have more competition in the next few months. Even if it does have a one-of-a-kind layout or a remodeled guest bathroom.

If the reverse is true and Months Supply is getting lower (for example January was 10, February was 9.5, March 9.2, April 8, and so on) a buyer's market is likely ending. Keep in mind, prices may get higher in the coming months. Frantic and rushed real estate purchases are never a good idea, but the tables could soon turn, so don't delay in doing the careful research today that will help you make solid, swift decisions.

Months Supply of 8 to 9: There are many homes for sale and sellers are having a tough time generating interest in their properties. If you're looking to buy a home, ask your realtor to print out the neighborhood's sales for the past three months. Then, when placing offers, make them 3 to 10 percent lower than what comparable properties in the neighborhood sold for a month before.

Sellers, prepare to receive slightly depressed bids and remember that *holding on* to your home costs money too— your mortgage and any related expenses.

Months Supply of 10 to 12: When it would take almost a year to sell all the homes on the market, there's a big supply. Buyers are in control. But by digging up fair, assessed values and offering the market-bottom rate you might actually make off like a bandit.

If you have no choice but to sell your home in this market, get yourself to a home improvement store, because a few do-it-yourself moves could help you beat the competition. First, paint your walls off-white or light beige, which is clean but not shocking like bright white, or distracting, like green. Then eliminate clutter (if it were only that easy . . .). File papers, stack towels in closets, and toss old and clunky extension cords and broken appliances. Sell or donate clunky furniture that's crowding rooms, particularly stand-alone file cabinets or extra sofas. Don't over-eliminate; you'll need a few clean pieces so prospective buyers can get the sense of space (stark empty rooms actually look smaller). Store under your bed or donate to your local library any books that are overflowing from shelves. While you're rummaging through reading material, don't forget to recycle that pile of magazines.

Do not drag everything into your garage. Prospective buyers look carefully there, so keep yours neat. Instead, store tools on shelves, throw away old bikes and anything else that will not only cost you the sale but also just mean more to move.

If selling your home, it's time to take a long look at your price and think about cutting it even deeper. Think about what *not* selling your house costs. Because carrying a property is expensive—your mortgage payment plus lawn care, electricity—it all adds up. Remember that even in slow-selling times, well-priced homes have been snatched up quickly.

Months Supply of 5 or Lower— a Seller's Market (Owners Hold the Power)

Months Supply of 5 or Lower: Sellers can get top dollar for their properties. Buyers are shopping, aware they have to be aggressive, and scooping up homes at prices that hover around what owners are asking, not much lower. If you're selling, that's great news. Your home, unless haunted, should get solid offers. If it doesn't, realize you've probably been possessed with greed and have overpriced the property.

Buyers, beware. You may be in the market to purchase a property because you just sold your ex-home for a fortune. Ka-ching. But your profits are at this point going into someone else's pocket. Check the Affordability Index and make sure that it's not a dangerous time to be home-buying.

If it is, strategize a plan. Can you rent until prices soften? Or can you move to a less expensive market where homes experienced more modest price gains?

Tina, a real estate broker who sold her home in Boca Raton, Florida, for $1.2 million, is a good example. Rather than spend her $800,000 profit on pricey real estate, she relocated her family to Greenville, South Carolina. There, prices were slightly elevated but hadn't experienced the same jolts they had back home. She got a bigger home by spending less than half her money. The rest went right to the bank.

Months Supply of 3 to 4: Real estate markets are white-hot. If you're still determined to buy, be warned you're doing so at a market high. Also remember that you might have to make a swift offer or lose the property. Do your homework in advance, learning about the school options, commute to work, and taxes so when paying those high prices at least you know what else you're getting.

STEP 3: BUYING IN THE RIGHT PLACE

In every real estate market, one mantra is consistent: location, location, location. It's frequently recited when describing the three criteria necessary for a property to be a good investment.

That's because it's true.

Favorable market forces are certainly helpful, but local communities can buck national trends. Some small real estate markets do very well during downturns. Others depreciate even though most markets are rising. After looking at the overall direction of the market, zoom in on hyper-local neighborhoods and assess the strength. The most reliable information can be gathered firsthand. Speak to locals, read newspapers, drive around and consider conditions such as lawn maintenance, shop closings, community bustle, parks, and schools. Does everything look clean and well maintained?

But there's also economic data to assist: the unemployment rate, which is the percent of the labor market actively looking for jobs but unable to find them. Real estate values can be affected by a local unemployment rate. Students and stay-at-home moms are not considered unemployed, as they're not counted as part of the labor market (despite the latter group experiencing labor painful enough to require medication). The labor market is made up only of two groups: those who are employed and those who are actively looking to be employed. Too much unemployment in your neighborhood will lower your own property value. Speaking of property, home taxes tend to fund community services, such as schools and parks. The people without jobs have trouble paying taxes, and those people could struggle to cofund the very places your kids learn and play.

The national unemployment rate is on the home page of the Labor Department's website (www.bls.gov). Monthly, the Labor Department also calculates the percent of people in thousands of communities who want jobs but can't find them. Local Area Unemployment Statistics (LAUS) are also available on the Bureau of Labor Statistics website (www.bls.gov/lau).

Scroll down to Databases, then select One Screen Data Search. In the dropdown boxes, first choose your state and then, in the next selection, choose cities and towns with a population of more than twenty-five thousand. The system will spit out a long list of numbers. You need only the unemployment rate for the most recent date provided. It will be in the upper right-hand corner of the table. Find the one you're considering and see how the local rate compares to unemployment in the country. If the local rate is higher, it means unemployment is more of a problem in this town than in the country as a whole. It makes the property values riskier. If the unemployment rate is lower, more people in that town have jobs than compared to the nation as a whole.

Example:

National Rate

- 5.9 percent

Arizona

- El Mirage City: 7.9 percent
- Queen Creek Town: 5.1 percent
- Mesa City: 4.7 percent
- Scottsdale: 3.8 percent

Shopping for a home in Arizona, a person could conclude that Scottsdale, where such a small percentage of people want jobs but don't have them, has a better chance of surviving an economic downturn. And that in El Mirage City, even a big home could depreciate in value. There, a big percent of people want jobs but can't find them. Without incomes, local property tax revenues—which fund schools, parks, and police—are weak. And property values could be following suit.

CHAPTER FOUR

Schools

choose
PUBLIC SCHOOL
OVER PRIVATE EDUCATION

Save Estimated $325,926

The Stuff You'll Skip

If the tuition is $15,000 a year, and that amount was invested each year, in the same account, over ten years you would have nearly $250,000.

For $20,000-per-year tuition, that's around $325,000 over ten years.

And when tuition is $25,000 a year, you're missing on nearly $400,000 over ten years.

For one child.

Whe it came time to select a school for her kids, my friend Paulina could, with great conviction, recite all the reasons she chose a private education. The public school had mold. The classes were big. One teacher mispronounced the word *library* as "li-berry." The halls were dark. It looked like a prison. It wasn't easy for her to spend $24,000 for both her son and daughter to attend Catholic school. But public school was bad, she told both herself and her husband. Private school was where you sent your kids if you truly cared about education. This is what she believed.

Even if she didn't actually believe it.

Really, Paulina was delivering the mantras of her social circle, the chatter among parents. Many of them were accustomed to actively dismissing the idea of using their free, community-school counterpart. The most gracious of them would shrug and say it was probably just fine. The most insufferable would whisper tales of a "mold and asbestos waiver" parents were forced to sign. (It was actually an information sheet explaining that federal guidelines mandated the school be inspected every year for both materials.)

Paulina didn't for one moment fight the pressure. She instead for years insisted to her husband they pay up. Until they couldn't any longer. And they both finally found happiness ever after in—yes—the community's public school. Where she then started singing its praises and poking holes in the private school programs.

You might call that insecurity. But even the most confident among us—public or private school parents—will occasionally question the educational decisions we've made for our kids. It's an important choice, one we believe will determine our child's entire social and economic future. Not something we want to mess up.

And there are thousands of considerations—from language programs to lunches to school locations—that we'll factor in to our decisions. One of the hard parts is not figuring out what we want, but seeing what we give up.

Rarely does this uncertainty result in a calm deliberation among concerned grown-ups. On the contrary, the issue transforms otherwise pleasant, soccer-coaching, wine-drinking parents into the defensive protectors of a particular educational system. Sometimes they're hysterical and other times smug. Occasionally, there are social media posts. It's clear a person cannot assume Parental Superiority without the willingness to publicly insult her alternatives.

The only people who more frequently debate the issue than parents are economists. Teams of US government researchers and numerous other private industry social scientists have studied the effects of both school systems. They've scrutinized test scores and then scrutinized them again. They've compared the results in countless ways. It's safe to say that like parents, these researchers would argue on so many matters, perhaps even where to order lunch. But they can together make one collective statement: A child's academic success is most strongly tied to his parents' involvement in the matter.

After that, it's up in the air.

New powerful findings claim public schools are outperforming private schools. That's contrary to what most of the country—including the college professors who produced the results—had always believed. But what these researchers have shown is that if you compare test scores of groups of kids from the same social and economic status, the public school group outperforms the private school counterparts.

To be clear, if we're looking at overall averages, the scores of private school students are always higher than those of public school students. That's not particularly surprising or even, for that matter, revealing. Everyone knows private schools can select the kids they want to admit. And in doing so, they will choose the students who are likely to make strong academic gains, before their parents have written a single tuition check. The question became, can we credit the schools for those progressively high scores?

At first, yes, that's exactly what we did. Sometime in the early 1980s, we as a nation agreed that private schools were better and neatly packaged those sentiments into what's called "The Private School Effect." Low-income parents struggled to afford tuition. Middle-class and rich kids enrolled without looking in another direction. And everyone else spent a decent amount of time rationalizing their decisions and explaining them.

Policy, in turn, followed suit. In 2001, Congress passed No Child Left Behind, which at first included vouchers. Those would allow kids in underperforming schools to use federal money to attend private schools or other public schools. That portion of the law was controversial, but today, voucher programs are available in many US cities. What's more, public educators put more resources to charter schools. Run by corporations—not governments—charter schools, and their proponents, promised great performance incentives. That's because parents were opting for these schools—rather than having been assigned to them—and would most certainly pull out their kids if they didn't see great progress. Since 2000, charter schools went from comprising 1.7 percent to 5.8 percent of all public schools. The total number of them increased from 1,500 to 5,700. And the number of students enrolled in them went from 0.3 million to 2.1 million.[1]

Like many great discoveries proving an entire country wrong, it was by accident that two researchers produced evidence they say suggests the opposite: Public schools are superior. Husband and wife team Sarah Theule Lubienski and Christopher Lubienski from the University of Illinois were studying mathematics instruction and looking at achievement data, when, for fun (which clearly has a different meaning to mathematics instructors), they started playing with the data. And found public school kids had better scores.[2]

They imposed some restrictions (controls, they're called), meaning the professors simply compared the performance levels of students from the same economic and ethnic backgrounds. Instead of comparing public school students to private school students, they compared rich public school students to rich private school students, as both types of schools had similar student bodies when it came to not only money but also ethnicity and language. They did the same with poor public school students and poor private school students. They compared urban schools to each other, and rural schools. They compared apples to apples.

A lot goes into an apple's production. There are weather conditions, travel distance from farm to market, method of transport, and pesticides used. If all of Farm A's apples are gorgeous but sprayed in pesticides, and only some of Farm B's apples are gorgeous and only some get treated, do we credit the farm? Or the pesticide? To fairly compare things (schools, apples, jeans), statisticians use a process called regression analysis. If you think that sentence was boring, wait until you find out it involves words such as *ameliorates* and *hierarchical linear modeling*. Regardless, it's a process that tells you how strong a relationship exists between a particular factor and a particular outcome.

In this case, "academic achievement" was the outcome the Lubienskis were studying. And they wanted to know what caused it, so they looked at fourth-grade and eighth-grade math scores (math, as opposed to languages, is something they say is generally taught exclusively at school) from the National Assessment of Educational Progress mathematics exam. They wanted to know why private schools were scoring so high. Was it great teachers? Small class sizes? Organization? Was it because private schools are free of the bureaucracy and political entanglements?

Nope. None of that.

Actually the Lubienski team went on to issue surveys they used in their book, *The Public School Advantage*.[3] And they found private schools *could* use their autonomy from federal regulations to embrace experimental and cutting-edge curriculums. But they don't. Instead the responses the Lubienskis got indicated that private schools frequently use their freedom to hold on to outdated strategies and tired curriculums. Their students were more likely than public schools to sit in rows and complete math worksheets, the Lubienskis say. Private school culture meant that math was mostly memorization.

The Lubienski team surmises that a private school's competitive quest for students—customers, really—puts them at a disadvantage. First, many stick to the instructional methods that please parents. Even if they're tired and ineffective, they're familiar to the people writing the tuition checks, the Lubienskis say. And second, private school teachers may not even know about some of the latest educational strategies because their employers put dollars toward marketing, not educational conferences.

Public school teachers, on the other hand, are more likely to be certified and most are required to receive ongoing training—something that's positively associated with student academic achievement, the Lubienskis write. Public school students had moved beyond "traditional repetitive exercises" and on to complex, real world problems. Even at the earliest years, at the introduction of basic arithmetic, the kids also learn geometry, data analysis, and early algebra. Public school teaching is more aligned with critical thinking.

So why are public school kids getting lower scores? Demographics. These students are more likely to be at risk, meaning public school enrollment includes more disabled and poor students. Poor kids aren't dumb, of course. But their parents—in the best of circumstances—tend to be more focused on buying food than, say, cutting out news articles their kids might find interesting. They have fewer books at home in a collection that's not typically updated. Poor kids are less likely to have access to a computer and the Internet. The high scores of private school kids are thanks to what happens not in the classroom but at home, say the Lubienskis.

Those results got a lot of attention and not all of it was applause. But about a year later, researchers from the Center on Education Policy came out with a paper called "Are Private Schools Better Academically Than Public High Schools?"[4] Most of us on the sidelines of soccer fields are not equipped to measure future happiness, but researchers at the CEP totally are. Using something called longitudinal data, which monitors the same kids at different points in time, they compared public and private school kids beginning in eighth grade until age twenty-six. Sure, they looked at academic advancement and college completion, but also two important postcollege measures of fulfillment: job satisfaction and civic involvement.

The CEP pulled aside thirteen thousand of the country's poor, urban eighth graders and got their personal information: school experience, home experience, plans for later education and life. The students were tested and retested throughout their school years. They were also surveyed, as were their teachers, principals, and parents. The private school kids—as usual—scored higher. And there was one noticeable advantage among them: They got better SAT scores. That means they were admitted to more elite universities. The famous Private School Effect did most certainly exist.

But when it came to academic advancements in senior year, the advantage of going to a private school disappeared. What mattered more was whether parents discussed schoolwork with their children and helped with assignments at home. It mattered whether parents had high expectations for their children, as researchers find that many public school parents set the bar at two-year colleges. The private school parents also offer an advantage the researchers call "Cultural Capital," which is the academic way of saying they have experiences that some kids can't afford. They went to museums, took music lessons, participated in academic enrichment experiences, and discussed world issues with their parents. They stored this stuff up in their heads and drew on it later, in their classes and on assessments.

What did not matter was whether the kid went to public school or private school. It was the high-quality parenting: Those free at-home conversations pushed up the scores. Not the schools.

When these kids turned twenty-six, they were interviewed again. The more college a kid completed, the more money the kid made. The high school attended didn't make a difference. While education played a large role in a person's civic involvement as an adult, it had to do with quantity. The more schooling a person had, the more likely that person was to be involved in the community at twenty-six years old. Young adults with high grades in high school civics classes were also more likely to be involved. But private school did not better prepare students to be civic-minded.

Nothing could predict whether a person had high job satisfaction. The researchers admit perhaps there's no difference between public and private when it comes to that particular metric. Perhaps the methods they employed were ineffective at measuring this factor. Straight from the researchers: "The private school advantage is a chimera: It merely shows that private schools contain a larger proportion of children whose parents have characteristics that contribute to learning than public schools. Students who attend private high schools receive nether immediate academic advantages nor longer term advantages in attending college, finding satisfaction in the job market, or participating in civic life."

Well, to say findings like those were debated and discredited is an understatement. Several competing studies came out, not necessarily saying that private schools were better, but that you just can't use some of this data to make the determination.

In the midst of it all, a study from the US Department of Education proved the public school superiority in at least fourth-grade math—but Harvard researchers Paul E. Peterson and Elena Llaudet disputed the work.[5] The first problem, says the Harvard team, was that the study underestimated the number of poor kids in private school, meaning this study didn't compare apples to apples at all. Private schools don't, say the Harvard professors, apply for federal dollars targeted for poor kids. And federal funding, they point out, was an important tool used to measure how many of those kids are in public schools. But since there was no federal funding given to private schools, poor kids went underrepresented there. Had these kids been accounted for, the results would prove a Private School Effect.

The Harvard researchers also say that while, sure, studies show how parenting affects the outcome in schooling, they don't measure the reverse: how school policy affects parenting. For example, parents can ensure their kids go to school each day. But what about attendance rules and tardy policies? Don't those affect parents' behavior? Academic requirements, assignments, and parent conferences all could reasonably affect what happens at home.

I, for one, am not going to argue with Harvard researchers. It's pretty difficult for most of us to debate which study has the most credibility with any real authority. But even *these* researchers say their work doesn't prove private schools are better. Only that the other studies don't prove the opposite, the public school advantage.

And that's the point here: No one has proof that you must pay private school tuition in order for your child to excel in life. Not the researchers, and not me, though I will take this opportunity to share a personal experience.

My children were enrolled in a $6,000-a-year preschool beginning at eighteen months that fed into its own $15,000-a-year elementary school. My kids were considered among those who would enroll for many reasons. Most notably, perhaps, because I'd filled out their applications and paid the deposit. So sure, understandable.

What was less so were the remarks some other parents made when I announced at the last minute that my oldest would instead go to a public school bilingual program, which was close enough to home she could walk! It started with a slow simmer. When I dropped off our youngest at the preschool, at least one other parent raised her eyebrows at our new car—our lease was up; it was a new car or nothing—and whispered perhaps we were squandering away our educational dollars in favor of status purchases. There were a few other comments, including questioning of my public school decision when I could afford to do better for my kids, and the occasional implication that my kids were out of the running for admission to the area's most competitive—and private—middle school.

My oldest daughter was admitted instantly to the private middle school; the other one didn't apply, opting instead for its rival. Our acquisition of status items remained unchanged, meaning there should be more interesting topics around here to discuss. And both of my girls are fluent in Spanish. To be fair, neither of them walked to school even once. That would have meant being ready ten minutes earlier, which is apparently more difficult than learning a foreign language.

In light of it all, we can send our kids to private school, but we cannot send them there to validate the philosophies of our friends or neighbors—people who have never even run a regression analysis. As parents, we now have prominent educators waving their research, arguing on our behalf that it doesn't cost a fortune to produce highly educated, academically advanced children. At least two of them are saying the paid route has barriers many hadn't considered. But everyone knows there are benefits and opportunities everywhere, and not only in exchange for tuition. The free stuff can win if we apply strong parenting. And think about it: That's required if you pay for private school *anyway*.

Raise Them Better for Less

Choosing a school is a personal choice and, for some parents, a difficult one. A child's education is arguably the single most important input to his or her upbringing. School is where kids are influenced intellectually and socially. Oh, and fashionably, which by junior high can get pretty scary.

Despite conflicting research and test scores proving one system is superior, all the experts agree that the foundation for great academic advancement is built at home. They say involved parenting—and maybe a few piano lessons—are most likely to produce the results we all want: high-achieving kids. Conveniently, involved parenting is the more affordable notion.

To help everyone—public and private school parents—you'll find here the Best of Both Worlds, shining stars of each educational system. Alongside, there's expert advice we can use to supplement our kids' schooling so we can all have it all. There's also plenty of facts we can use to arm ourselves with the information we'll need to feel good about paying tuition. Or not paying tuition.

1. GREAT EXPECTATIONS

Researchers from the Center for Education Policy found that public school kids completed less college than private school kids because their parents expected them to complete less college.[6] Not because they weren't prepared. The lesson? Set a high educational bar beginning at age five, says Bill Jackson, CEO of GreatSchools. This does not mean withholding chicken fingers until the kid promises to get a doctorate in nuclear physics. Rather, says Jackson, we should simply work into conversations sentences such as *When you go to college . . .* Our kids, he says, should grow up assuming that they'll be attending four-year universities. By the time they're fifteen years old, they may start to consider their interest and whether those goals will require graduate school. But for now, between kindergarten and middle school, Jackson says we should help them internalize high expectations by rewarding results and effort.

2. PARENT INVOLVEMENT

Remember, achievement is highest in kids whose parents are involved in their schoolwork. If you've ever gotten involved in a science project, only to be interrupted by your child asking if *she* could please help *you*, you know it's possible to overdo things in this department. While *involvement* has a different definition at every stage, it never means doing the work yourself, says Jackson. In kindergarten or first grade—whenever they start getting homework—we should schedule the same time each day for school assignments and set aside a quiet place to tackle them, says Jackson. By middle and high school, this should become habit and our involvement turns into interest, making studies the subject of dinnertime conversation. "If you look at parents who are supportive of their kids' education, they're engaging them with ideas, talking about what's going on in the world. They treat them like little adults."

3. CLASS SIZE CONSIDERATION

Private schools have smaller classes (numbers below). Does that equal better? Sometimes. Smaller classes are highly beneficial for early literacy and children with developmental delays, says Jackson. In other instances, such as in writing labs, smaller class sizes allow teachers to more carefully and thoughtfully grade papers. But Jackson also points to scores of findings—including those from Stanford University economist Caroline M. Hoxby[7]—showing that, as early as fourth grade, smaller class sizes have no impact on test scores. Jackson would rather schools aim to have large classes taught by interesting and highly engaging teachers.

Number of Students per Teacher (projections)[8]		
	Public	Private
2013	16.0	12.5
2021	15.4	12.1

You can easily research class size in your school—public or private—and compare class sizes between schools and states by going to http://nces.ed.gov/globallocator. You can compare your school to others by typing the names into the database or to statewide averages that are updated by the National Center for Education Statistics. A sample of the facts you'll find:

Information

- **Institution Name:** Adelle Turner El
- **Institution Type:** Public School
- **District:** Dallas Isd
- **County:** Dallas County

Characteristics

- **Locale:** City: Large (11)
- **Type:** Regular school
- **Charter:** no
- **Magnet:** no
- **Total Teachers (FTE):** 29.00
- **Total Students:** 419
- **Student/Teacher Ratio:** 14.45

Enrollment by Grade
Grade Levels: PK - 05**

- **PK:** 34
- **KG:** 52
- **1st Grade:** 57
- **2nd Grade:** 59
- **3rd Grade:** 61
- **4th Grade:** 87
- **5th Grade:** 69

**(PK = PreKindergarten KG = Kindergarten)

(Source: CCD Public school data 2011–12 school year)

4. TEACHER TALKS

Parent-teacher conferences happen more frequently in private schools, where 85 percent of parents regularly attend[9]—the other 15 percent is likely spouses (possibly husbands) who have gotten quite skilled at tuning out such reminders. That's compared to some 75 percent of public school parents. There is no data about how frequently each system offers the conferences, but it's fair to assume that in some public schools, the extra school days—and therefore teacher pay—they require are killed in steep budget cuts (one day of pay for some twenty thousand teachers adds up . . .).

The most important aspect of these conferences—aside from actually showing up—is to walk away with a clear understanding of your child's strengths and weaknesses, says Jackson. And to learn actionable steps you can take to make your child more successful.

5. SPECIALIST INVESTIGATIONS

More public elementary schools—63.1 percent of them—have an academic specialist working with students or a coaching specialist to support teachers. In private schools, only 36.5 percent have one or both of those on staff. That's because public schools, says Jackson, typically have more infrastructure positions for teacher and student support.

Sometimes, however, those positions are located on site or in central, district offices. When there is an instructional focus on either helping students or improving teaching quality and school leadership, says Jackson, these positions can have a very positive impact on the academic experience. But that's not always the case, he says. Sometimes, the instruction is phoned in or not passed along at all. Investigate by asking not only whether there's a specialist assigned to the school, but also about the methods for that professional to critique or observe the classes.

6. TEACHER TERMS

There are all sorts of stats about teachers moving jobs—they're below—but the bottom line is public school teachers tend to stay around longer. Does that make a difference? The best possible scenario in schools, says Jackson, is a healthy mix of new teachers and seasoned ones. "If you have a school full of fresh teachers, they may be reinventing the wheel," he says. "While the teachers who have been around a while won't typically offer new ideas."

Percent of Teachers Staying at and Leaving Their Schools, 2007–2008 School Year

	Public	Private
Remained at same school the following year[10]	84.5%	79.2%
Left profession	8%	15.9%
% of contracts not renewed	5%	13%
Moved to a different school	7.6%	4.9%
Left for personal life factors	26.2%	16%

7. EDUCATING THE EDUCATORS

Public schools have more teachers with graduate degrees—52 percent had a master's degree or higher compared to 38 percent of teachers in private schools, says the NCES. There is, however, some question about whether this matters, and by "some question" I mean a raging debate throughout America. It's causing scores of economists to warn that paying extra money to teachers with master's degrees is a waste of perfectly good educational funding. Matthew Chingos of the Brookings Institution wrote that he studied student achievement of the same teachers before and after they earned master's degrees and noticed zero difference.[11]

8. PAYSCALE COMPARISONS

Public school teachers make more money, which shouldn't mean anything— seeing as a person who pursues teaching for the money is crazy and shouldn't be working around young children. The average annual base salary of regular full-time public school teacher was $49,600, and $36,300 for a private school teacher at last count in 2008, says the NCES.

9. CULTURAL CAPITAL

An important influence on the high test scores of private school students was "Cultural Capital,"[12] such as museum visits and dinnertime discussions on current events and music lessons. When surveyed, about 20 percent of public school families (9.4 million kids) had visited an art gallery, museum, or historical site in the past month, while 25 percent of private school families (800,000 kids) reported going, says NCES.[13]

See, that proves it: You can get Cultural Capital in public school too. Without the private school tuition you can have the Cultural Capital part pump up your kids' test scores. What's more, most museums have a free admission day each month. Historic sites rarely have fees and typically they're small. The problem—let's assume for most people—is that sports, school, and social occasions get in the way of our very grand Cultural Capital plans. Calendar them in advance and consider the appointment unbreakable. Done.

Newspapers are under $2 and scanning them for interesting articles takes nine minutes. Do that once a week and find a topic for dinnertime discussion. You may find a free cultural event for kids.

As for music lessons, playing an instrument can help with math skills. Group classes offer the least expensive instruction. Can't find one in your community? Even better. Hit the local college in search of a music major who needs extra cash (and unless you come across a student with the last name Estefan, that should describe many music majors) and strike a deal. It'll go something like: "I'm organizing a guitar class for nine-year-olds. I'll bring ten kids, charge them each $30 a session, and mine attends for free. Deal?"

10. THE SAT SITUATION

Even public school advocates agree: Private college prep schools are better at preparing kids for the SAT tests that heavily impact college admissions. Take a look:

SAT Scores, US Average vs. Independent School Average		
	US Average	Independent School Average
Critical Reading	497	588
Math	513	603
Writing	487	589

(Source: National Association of Independent Schools)

These results show up in the admissions statistics of the nation's top colleges. While a bigger portion of each incoming class tends to come from public high school, the private school students still make up a glaringly large slice of the Competitive College Pie. Consider: Less than 2 percent of the nation's high school students are enrolled in private school, and yet they made up 38 percent of Dartmouth's most recent incoming class and 45 percent of Yale's. Having legacy—not to mention a few bucks—can't possibly hurt. But even so, you've got to have the SAT scores.

What's nice is that the very same people who write the SAT questions are also gearing up to better help kids study. The College Board admits there's inequity in the test. So it has partnered with Khan Academy to create interactive software that helps kids prepare—for free. What's more, the College Board website (www.collegeboard. org) has online courses, free practice tests, and free sample questions, which are both addictive and pretty hard.

Admission Stats from a Few Top Schools, Class of 2018

	Public	Private	Parochial	Homeschooled
Dartmouth	57%	38%	—	6%
Yale	55%	45%	—	—
Princeton	59.2%	28%*	12%	0.6%
Cornell	64.6%	18%	—	—
Duke	60%	33.5%**	—	—
Stanford	60.2%	29.7%	—	0.4%
Harvard	67%	33%	—	—

* 19.2% (independent + 8.8% (boarding)   ** includes religious schools and homeschooled)

(Source: Dartmouth.edu, Yale.edu, Princeton.edu, Cornell.edu, Duke.edu, Stanford.edu; Harvard, email from Anna Cowenhoven, Director, University Communications)

11. CREDIT COUNSELING

If you look at the National Assessment of Educational Progress scores, private school scores are higher than public school scores, but some researchers say that's because public schools enroll more at-risk kids—those who are disadvantaged economically, physically, or mentally. The effect quite possibly also surfaces in the portion of the kids completing high-level courses. Stay on top of your kids by knowing what's happening everywhere. Private school students on average graduate with more science credits: 3.6 as opposed to 3.3 for public school students, says the NCES. In 2004, 28 percent of private school students (some 896,000 kids) progressed through the science pipeline to the highest level compared to 18 percent of public school students (8,460,000 students). And enrollment in calculus is higher at private schools.

Percentage of Students Taking Calculus		
	Public	Private
1994	5%	22.3%
2004	13%	30.7%

(Source: National Center for Education Statistics)

12. RESPONSE TIME

Private schools are more responsive to parents. About 78 percent of parents in private schools are happy with their interactions with teachers and staff. In public schools, 49 percent of parents said they were satisfied.[14] While many parents have great relationships with their public school teachers and principals, many do not. (When you're talking about 47 million anything, let alone *parents,* someone's going to be unhappy.) When it comes to *any* school, investing a little time in the classroom or on the PTA can have lasting effects on your relationship with the teachers, and that can spill over to help your children. That's even truer in public school, where if you supplement the education with some sweat hours, you're likely to find the teachers and principal more responsive. No one wants to spend a vacation day volunteering at a school bake sale, but everyone wants to have a personal relationship with the people educating their kids. There are typically creative

Percentage of Involvement in Schools[15]		
	Public	Private
Serving on a Committee	38	69
Participating in fund-raising	56	84

(Source: National Household Education Surveys Program, US Dept. of Education)

and hands-on solutions—staying to help out after drop-off, during your own extended lunch hour or working at weekend events such as carnivals and fairs. And they'll be viewed in the eyes of the school as helpful and therefore valuable. They will value you! And then *you'll* be the happier one for it.

Rock-Solid Money Move

Your Rock-Solid Money Move here is to give your kids cash. If that sounds counterproductive, then remember: Giving allowances is an excellent way to avoid buying things for our children. What's more, these payments will teach our kids money management. And like everything else, there is a different lesson for every age.

Our kids need to learn that money is critical for life. Even if acquiring things isn't your main focus, properly managing money is the only way people can achieve what is truly important to them. Musicians need to buy instruments, scientists need labs, writers need vodka, and everyone—no matter the profession—needs food, shelter, and health care. If securing any of those requires a struggle, then survival becomes a focus, and once-lofty goals take a back seat. What's more, doctors and business professionals and movie stars have all gone broke after failing to properly manage ample salaries.

We've got our work cut out for us. Only 9.4 percent of American fifteen-year-olds are financially literate in the highest sense, says the Organization for Economic Cooperation and Development.[17] That means they're able to understand how financial concepts may become relevant to their lives in the long term. The other 90 percent don't understand the potential outcomes of financial decisions, or the wider financial landscape, such as income tax.

It's never too early to start talking about money with our kids. We won't want to reveal our salaries—children are not known for their discretion—but from the time they're toddlers until they're teens, we can include them in everyday financial decisions. If we're discussing where to eat dinner, let the family collectively choose between a particular restaurant and less expensive restaurant plus a movie. Maybe everyone will vote to stay home, watch TV, and save the money for a dining extravaganza the following week. We have to teach our kids to be mindful of menu prices, even when we can easily afford the expense. The lesson isn't just in the luxury of eating out, but also in the art of socializing. Restaurant dining is an activity they'll do with grandparents and friends, who kindly extend invitations. The kid who goes to the pizza-salad occasion and orders the lobster fra diavolo is annoying.

You and your kids can compare prices everywhere. You don't have to teach them to always opt for the cheapest clothes or brands of paper towels (unless you're my husband and anything else goes against all that you know and believe). But you can introduce a mini quality-versus-price analysis, pointing out that there isn't always a tradeoff. Generic fruit cereal puffs are typically the same—if not even *fruitier*—than the brand-name version.

ARRIVAL OF THE ALLOWANCE

It's never too early to start giving our children allowances; some experts say if they're two years old, we're late. But coins are choking hazards, so it's with a hearty dose of neurosis that the recommendation here is age four. At that time, we should give the same monetary amounts each week but in different coin combinations—dimes one week, nickels another, then quarters—and explain the value of each. For the littlest kids, set up three containers: one labeled SAVINGS, which will get 10 percent of every allowance. One labeled DONATIONS, for charity or school fund-raisers. And one labeled SPENDING, for all the things at Target you typically refuse. That last one teaches that it takes a long time to accumulate enough money to get even one of the toys you want. And that once you do have the money, you have to choose between two or three very attractive options. (There's no need to explain that this is a struggle that continues well into middle age. Why depress the kid?)

The amounts of money you'll provide each week are discretionary and personal—basically you can just make it up. A great joy of parenting is the power to simply declare things based on your immediate mood. And then watching those whims become your kids' reality. (If you gave them unusual names, then you completely know what I'm talking about.) The only guideline to consider: Start small so there's room for an increase, which can also be completely invented— have fun with it!—or you can tie them to the inflation rate later on. Inflation is the increase in prices each year, and while your preschooler won't be ready for macroeconomics, everyone has an aging relative who frequently reports the price of a movie ticket when they were a kid. That's inflation, and little kids can understand the concept when you put it in understandable terms.

There is some debate about whether allowance money should be tied to chores, which would introduce the concept of working. But because the main goal is financial literacy—and not bed-making or room-cleaning (efforts you'd likely duplicate anyway)—it's also fine to tie these payments to the general responsibilities of childhood, such as completing homework, being on time for school, and not touching furniture with chocolate on your hands. This money, you should explain, is called income, and, as in the actual economy, the more education a person has, the more money she tends to earn. Joblessness is highest for those with just a high school degree. It's lowest for those with postsecondary graduate degrees. This is a good time to start the *When you go to college* . . . statements that GreatSchools CEO Bill Jackson suggested we make when setting high expectations.

SMART SPENDING AND SAVINGS

Each of us will decide what our young kids will buy themselves, though few of us are going to charge for breakfast cereal or winter heat. And while that's certainly your prerogative, the critical lesson to instill in children when comparing these items to sparkly hair accessories is need versus want. Needs are pretty much essential to survival—food, housing, education, health care. Wants are nice but not necessary. It's broccoli versus ice cream. School supplies versus movie tickets. I like my daughters to pay for their own school fund-raisers, particularly when it involves paying $1 to send each friend a message with a Valentine flower or any other tangible measure of popularity guaranteed to hurt someone's feelings.

Competition isn't only for receiving holiday messages; it's also an important part of the American economy. As soon as your kids start understanding commercials, you should explain that candymakers and toy companies and burger restaurants are all fighting for their dollars. In some ways, that's good for us customers. Companies know that if prices are unreasonable or if the quality is poor, we'll spend our money elsewhere. But also, companies desperate for our attention tend to exaggerate the greatness of what they're selling in their advertisements. Regardless of how good a snack tastes, we'll explain, no amount of powdered cheese can make a cartoon cheetah come to life in our living rooms. And the words *some assembly required* translates to "you'll be opening a box of seven million parts, kiddo." These companies, we'll tell our kids, are clamoring to get their messages in front of us by sponsoring our favorite television shows and buying space in the best magazines. They'll pay people—actors who look pretty or celebrities who sound genuine—to tell us a computer app made them smarter or a hamburger made them happier. Sometimes the sandwiches, they'll say, are healthier. But you have to ask your own questions: healthier than *what*? Probably nothing particularly healthy.

As our kids reach ages nine, ten, and eleven, they'll be ready to learn about choices. Because as both our own parents and also the nation's most esteemed economics professors will say, you cannot have everything. What you give up is called your "opportunity cost." And the two resources we'll be working with here are time and money. You cannot play outside and do homework during the very same minutes. You'll give one up for the other. And while you can on many days do both, you'll have to decide how to allocate those hours to maximize your grades and your free time, which is something you also don't want to waste on mean friends or boring television shows. Money and the things it can buy are more tangible. You can touch and see what you gain and what you give up. But don't forget to remind your kids that even in times they do get both items, they're still giving up the opportunity to save their money. In banks! That pay interest! That's the price of money, and the banks will pay you—you'll explain—to let them use your money for a little while. Savings accounts are the best place to earn interest, so now is a good time to open one up for your child. In your child's name.

TALKING STOCKS AND CREDIT

By around age ten, tiny bankers are ready to learn about the stock market. They won't need a subscription to *The Wall Street Journal* yet. But you should explain that regular people can buy ownership— called shares—into some very important companies, such as the McDonalds Corporation; Nike, Inc.; and Claire's Stores. When your kid likes shopping or eating at a company that's publicly traded, start talking about the product's quality and discuss how this might affect sales.

Shareholders make money when they buy the stock for a lower price than they sell the stock. The price of the stock will rise when the company sells lots of hamburgers, sneakers, or plastic jewelry (or even when the market believes it will soon sell lots). It falls when it sells less. Being a consumer is pretty powerful, we'll tell our kids. If you don't like the food or the service, you can make predictions, which is material for discussion when you're out.

At age eleven, it's time to circle back to inflation and those pesky price increases. You can illustrate price increases for things you both buy using what's nicknamed the "retail price" index but is actually called the consumer price index. You'll hear on business television just one number reported (the CPI, reporters will call it), but that's really an average of 372 items. Those individual price increases—lettuce, gas, cupcakes, salad dressing, movie admissions—are reported by the Bureau of Labor Statistics and also on TheHomeEconomist.com, where there's a Kids Consume table, which looks like this:

Price Increases for Kid Stuff

- Candy and chewing gum: up 1.9 percent
- Girls' apparel: up 3.2 percent
- Sporting goods: up 2.3 percent
- Toys: down 6 percent
- Musical instruments: up 3.2 percent
- Sports club fees: up 3 percent
- Admissions to movies, theaters, and concerts: up 1.8 percent
- Cosmetics: up 1.9 percent
- Wireless telephone: down 3.2 percent

By age twelve, your kids should know that credit cards are not money. And they're not magic. Credit cards are merely convenient, as it's dangerous to carry too much cash. Through these cards, we get loans from banks that, unfortunately, *charge* us a lot more interest than they're willing to *pay* through those savings accounts we opened. Even if you buy a toy on sale for 50 percent off, its price over time can double when you tack on the interest you'll have to pay by letting the loan lapse. (Tragically, a *child's* interest in the very same toy is guaranteed to *fall* in the opposite direction at an even faster rate.) Not paying your credit cards on time isn't only financially expensive; it can cost you future opportunities. In explaining credit reports to our kids by age twelve, we may want to first apologize for the Santa and Tooth Fairy thing before explaining there really are—we swear this time—agencies that know if you've been good or bad when it comes to bill-paying. Because unlike the time you denied eating your brother's fries when he went to the bathroom, there is an electronic record of this stuff.

A credit report, we'll explain, is the financial report card following each of us around for life. It's accessed by lenders, who are considering whether to give you money for cars, houses, or college educations. And also by prospective bosses, who have been known to take a peek before deciding whom to hire. Remind your son or daughter that the ability to move out and make your own rules depends *entirely* on keeping this document pristine. (If that doesn't motivate the kid to keep clean credit, I don't know what will.)

Just as we sit in the front seat of the car and teach our kids to drive, we should—just as terrifyingly—give them credit or debit cards. These are people who need to learn the laws of spending under our supervision. Remember, when they graduate college and get jobs, they're going to receive offer upon tempting credit card offer. And solid preparation is their only defense against major accidents. You'll teach them that this is the same as cash, but more convenient. You'll monitor their bills and if they go over the limits, you'll decide the consequences. Pay you back? Lose the card? (Parenting comes with so many options.) You can even decide what kind of card they carry. Credit cards provide the real-world experience of unlimited options with dire consequences, but that's a big step. Prepaid cards get them used to limits, as do debit cards. Just be careful with your personal information. Identity thieves—people who pretend to be you and use your personal information to get loans they don't repay—can also cause a big problem for our credit reports. As our kids start independently using the Internet, we have to warn them to never give out even an ounce of personal information. Names and schools and especially their birthdays are juicy little clues a thief can use to find out our children's addresses and social security numbers, open accounts, and destroy their good names.

TAKING STOCK ACTION AND INTEREST

Your teen may shun the idea of hanging out with you publicly but she may be just fine with you together buying publicly traded companies. You'll have to open a custodial account, but investing in stocks is a crash course in finance and economics. You'll together watch how economic indicators, such as the unemployment rate and the inflation rate, impact the markets. You'll teach your child to diversify, putting some money into bonds and savings or by investing in different industries. You'll read articles together and discuss your stocks over dinner.

By high school we can introduce the concept of compounding interest. Given that we're dealing with the attention span of a teenager, we can open with, "Want to hear how to get more money *without even doing anything?*" This should buy you a couple of minutes. Quickly explain that if you save your money in an account that accumulates interest more than once each year, the interest starts to amass interest and your money multiplies over time. With these accounts, saving a little for a long time is often more effective than saving a lot in a short time. If the kid is still sitting there, keep going. Pull out the Rule of 72. You take the number 72 and divide it by the interest rate. The answer is the number of years it takes to double your money.

For example:

Interest rate: 6 percent
72 ÷ 6 = 12
It takes twelve years to double your money.

Use this concept to illustrate the true cost of whatever the kid thinks she cannot live without. Not only do you pay the price on the tag, screen, or menu. You lose the interest you might have earned.

Hey, if the kid becomes a financial tycoon, he may even be able to take over some of your responsibilities. If so, deposit into your child's account money for them to carefully allocate across some expenses you had been previously micromanaging. Start small with weekly allotments for entertainment. And if he finds there's no money for movies because it was all spent on mocha drinks, well, quality time at home on Saturday is a small price to pay for a lifelong budgeting lesson. You can also do this for clothes and extracurricular activities. Collect receipts for *all* purchases, because everyone—from CEOs to members of Congress to people in the most rebellious age group— must document their expenses.

In all these lessons we'll have to be good role models, demonstrating we ourselves know the difference between *need* and *want* and using credit cards responsibly. Some of us will be faking it, but hey, fake it until you make it, right? Start practicing what we preach. Spend less than we earn. Pay ourselves first. Expect the unexpected expenses. Remember that shopping at convenience stores is expensive. And cars are more costly than their sticker prices, thanks to gas, insurance, and repairs. We'll tell our kids—and ourselves—that even the best sale prices still cost money. Some of this will stick, mistakes will be made, and lobster fra diavolo will be ordered. But we'll all get there.

CHAPTER FIVE

Your Star

choose

ENDURANCE

OVER NARCISSISM

Save Estimated $45,119

The Stuff You'll Skip

Private lessons for kids ages 3 to 8,
   at $35 per hour: $6,350

Two lessons per month for older kids,
   over two years: $1,820

Professional equipment for two years: $500

Professional video production: $5,000

Total Cash Outlay: $13,670
Total Invested Savings after 18 years: $46,203

These days, one way to increase your chances of becoming a pop star is to appear on a televised talent competition. But when sixteen-year-old Danielle Bradbery won the *The Voice* and the corresponding recording contract with Republic Records, she later told reporters she'd never had any formal vocal training.

So did I feel stupid for spending $150 an hour on private singing lessons for my nine-year-old daughter? For a minute, maybe. But I have a very solid defense. First, for your information, I'm not trying to raise a pop star. I'd hired that particular coach after a less expensive instructor with whom we'd been working canceled a lesson due to the arrival of her menstrual period—setting back not only my day but also the entire women's movement.

I'm not a Stage Mom, you see. I'm *not* an overbearing woman who's forcing her kid to perform in order to satisfy some complicated feelings of my own. I'm simply a feminist who appreciates people keeping their appointments.

Right?

"Well, maybe," says Mark Hyman, a George Washington University professor who studies kids' sports and the author of *Until It Hurts* and *The Most Expensive Game In Town*. "But let's talk about how you might feel six years from now—after spending over $6,000—if your daughter comes home, sits you down, and genuinely no longer wants to sing. Could you be dispassionate about her singing career?"

Shit.

Suddenly, me becoming an overbearing woman forcing a kid to perform thanks to some complicated feelings of her own—in this case an emotional attachment that developed from a financial investment—isn't the *wildest* notion I'd ever heard. And the potential for my resenting her, followed by the potential for her to resent my resentment, not to mention the potential for her to resent singing, isn't even among the worst of potential outcomes. There's more. See, Hyman—who is an expert on the methods the most seemingly concerned coaches, companies, and even communities use to gently coerce dollars from our wallets—says our genuine steps toward what we believe are our kids' best interests can create "parenting dysfunction." It can happen to parents with kids involved in nearly any discipline or extracurricular activity—tennis, volleyball, singing, ballet, piano, lacrosse, drama, violin, sculpting, baseball, football, golf. But because a handful of sports players and stage performers become superstars, with great fame and huge amounts of money, it's exaggerated in these circles.

Even the most intense of us are not bad people or even bad parents, says Hyman. In fact, on the contrary, all of us are probably interested in keeping our kids active because we're well versed in the statistics showing obesity plagues 18 percent of American children.[1] And sure, our hearts are full when listening to our kids sing or play piano, but we're also aware that music lessons are positively tied to academic performance.

That's what the experts tell us. But they don't advise much further, so we turn to coaches and music teachers, equipment salespeople and advice counselors, all of whom, we believe, know better than us. And each of whom profit from our parenting pursuits. It's not that they don't truly believe their discipline is important. They love their craft, they love our kids, and they're competitive—they promise us that. But one fact we can't deny: The more money we spend, the more they make. These teachers and coaches dangle in front of us carrots of high achievement. We'll hear of former students who were awarded athletic scholarships, and we watch videos of kids singing on Broadway and *American Idol*. They tout catchphrases such as *maximize your potential* and promise higher self-esteem and better social skills. They drop names and post on their website quotes from

Japanese musician Shinichi Suzuki, saying that children who hear fine music will develop sensitivity, discipline, and endurance.

We salivate.

Self-esteem? High achievement? Social skills? We're starving for our kids to have these qualities. If self-esteem is for sale, we're prepared to buy it. *Take our money. Our cash has no better use. Also put on our tab whatever registration fees or equipment are necessary.* This is what parenting is about.

One father confessed to Hyman that, in order to pay for his son's golf lessons, tournament fees, and related expenses, he at times skipped making payments for the family's health insurance. Online, a mother confided to the readers of Mommyish.com she was spending $300 an hour for her daughter's singing lessons and hiding the entire endeavor from her husband. A blogger who calls himself Stats Dad calculated he'd shelled out $11,704 one year on his kids' sports career for items including Nike cleats for $90 and fees such as the condo basketball tournament that charged $1,600. There are baseball bats for $300, but they last only one season. Sure, you can buy lacrosse sticks for just $40, but—my friend Denise informed me last week—the $200 versions have wider nets and swiveling heads. Her son, she said with the unmistakable air of superiority, "got competitive" and now owns that stick. I got the feeling I was supposed to be impressed. Nikki and Louis Jackson, meanwhile, who live in a suburb of Washington, DC, where the median income is $38,000, told Marketplace.org[2] they're counting heavily on their kids earning athletic scholarships. To that end, they're investing in this with personal trainers and $179 baseball bats. "It's a big difference from a $40, $50 bat," Louis Jackson told reporter Scott Tong. "It's a *big* difference, man." And that's one where you say, as he does, "You've got to pay to play."

These are not one-time expenses, but accumulative and reccurring, year after year. Equipment wears from use, takes a beating, gets lost, then must be replaced. After putting this much time and money into the whole endeavor, are you really going to let the kid lose by one point for not having the advantage of a swiveling lacrosse net? Hyman bets not.

Here's where the problems only begin. We're happy with our coaches and their progress, mostly because we see results. We consider the long-run potential. It's not long before we're approaching these kids' activities as we would our own adult interests: with a more-is-better mentality, says Hyman. If we go to the gym more, we'll lose weight faster. If we go to the office earlier, we'll make more money. If our kid has more coaching, she'll have more wins. She'll get more roles. More chances to shine.

Deep down, we all know the truth: Real winners in youth sports learn sportsmanship and make friends. They figure out how to work on a team and develop a lifelong appreciation for physical fitness. In drama or music, it's not necessarily the star of the play who shines forever, but rather the kid who learns how to prepare for a production or the one who gains confidence by performing in front of an audience. The long-term benefits come from learning to manage stage fright and developing a solid work ethic for meeting deadlines.

But too often, warns Hyman, the star doesn't get the long-term benefits. The kid may early on display a talent in a particular sport (say baseball) while playing on the fall team. Soon that kid is recruited to the winter travel team. Registration fees can run $3,000 and that's before the travel expenses of several two-day trips including hotels and food. What's more, most teams chip in for the coach's travel expenses. After that, this talented athlete will be recommended for a specialty summer camp. There's a strong likelihood as to what will unfold next, says Hyman. First, spectators in the stands will applaud this kid's abilities, his teammates will cheer, and the coaches will clamor. This child will continue to train, probably harder.

Sometime after that, this star in sports or on stage runs the risk of two dark statistics: The first is that 50 percent of sports injuries among children come from overuse. Not, mind you, from sliding into first base. That's bad luck. But kids who put enormous strain on the same muscles can injure those muscles, such as when a child strains a rotator cuff from throwing with the same arm, over and over and over until the muscles can no longer support the shoulder joint and its ability to produce coordinated movements. A child's body cannot take the same stress as an adult's body. Strain on a bone, ligament, or tendon can not only ruin a kid's performance on the field, but also impair growth, cause chronic pain into adulthood, or even prevent the kid from proper use of whatever muscle or joint he or she managed to obliterate on your dime.

So your sports or stage star made it without injury? Kids who are living and breathing their activity are even more likely to fall into the second unfortunate stat: 70 percent of all kids drop out of their favorite sport before age thirteen, says Hyman. They're tired, bored, disinterested, defeated, whatever. Some attrition is normal. But because the leagues are constructed for the most competitive kids, the ones who want to play for fun are squeezed out, says Hyman. And it's that ratio that prompted Hyman to ask me right up front, you might remember, how I'd react if my kid decided to stop singing.

"The difficult line we walk as parents is to figure out if the money we're spending and the time we're spending is to support our child's interest or feed some emotional need of our own," says Hyman. None of us as parents, he swears, are 100 percent on one side or the other. It's a spectrum. Even during even our darkest moments, we'd never sacrifice our child's best interests for the sole purpose of furthering our own. But while our kids are winning, singing, or starring and we are beaming with pride, a tiny portion of that accomplishment is fueling our own lunacy. That's part of what drives us to pay for lessons and police the practicing. Because during these moments no one can argue: We've done something right.

Problem is, the very second we make parenting about our interests, and not our kids' interests, the child gets resentful. It's true, we all live with a little resentment. But when our kids internalize theirs, because we've told them exactly what they're going to do, resentment can lead to anger, guilt, or shame, says Miami-based family psychologist Netta Shaked. What's more, spending money on lessons and equipment is really wasted on a resentful kid. They don't perform at the same levels as those who are intrinsically motivated. They'll be less committed, and it's obvious in the outcome.

Parents, coaches, and companies may ask you to invest in those outcomes. Meet a new breed of American business: companies that are prepared and equipped to capture your hard work—wait, sorry, we mean *your child's* hard work—on video, in exchange for over $5,000. They will produce a package in which this kid freaking shines. She'll look gorgeous, he'll be a heartthrob, and everyone will perform to athletic or aesthetic perfection.

Athletes are told that if you want between $50,000 and $100,000 in scholarships, college recruiters need more than your athletic profile. You need to demonstrate your abilities on camera, complete with testimonials from coaches and teachers about your persistence and your personality. You cannot count on these recruiters to have the travel budget to stop in your city. But these companies, and there are dozens, will send your video directly to their offices. It's true, according to Hyman, who has seen those very same videos in dozens of offices, piled high in corners. These consultancy services start at $795, but some families spend as much as $5,000.

Similarly, record labels are waiting to sign stars—why not your kid? To get you started, Patrice Wilson will make a music video of your potential pop star, but you'll have to audition (a velvet rope is an effective way to produce desire) for the opportunity to pay him between $2,000 and $8,000. Wilson told the *Los Angeles Times*, "I'm getting a lot of criticism saying I'm exploiting rich kids and their parents. But find me another company that would do all this at a cost this low. I'm not in this to make millions. I just want to help these kids make their dreams come true on some level."[3]

I won't suggest that parents shouldn't help their kids reach for the highest star, despite the research that advises the contrary. I also won't suggest we don't make videos of our children. It just means that these expenses—if you cannot afford them—offer zero guarantees *and* a potential downside. I will take the advice of the skeptics and pass along the warning that these emotional and financial investments require due diligence or, in layman's terms, a severe reality check. Yes, there's potential here to win big. But if we do not have the disposable income for expensive coaching or packaging, we'll have to remember all the kids—*The Voice* winner Danielle Bradbery for starters—who achieved their dreams without professional videos or even lessons. Your kid may become a star without the video. Your kid may *not* become a star with the video. I don't know a person's chances for musical stardom. But only 5 percent of varsity high school athletes play in college, with just a sliver of them getting scholarships, says Hyman. And, by opting for these professional services, not only do our bank accounts get hit, but so do our kids' mental states.

You see, while there's certainly a potential upside to cultivating our kids' talents, there's also a potential downside: emotional expense. We've spent *years* paying professionals to prop up our kids. Yes, they correct missteps, but they also cheer on our children with the kind of encouragement that fuels our desire to pay for more lessons. While our kids are in full earshot, we'll discuss with these coaches their exceptional abilities. The coach's tone implies this is a fact. And now? We've spent $5,000 on a video of this child appearing flawless, performing on target, with any mistakes or unflattering moments edited out, as though they never existed. This video is very real to everyone involved.

So is narcissism, people.

Today, 30 percent more college-age kids will give narcissistic answers on personality tests than their counterparts in 1982, says Jean Twenge, author of *Generation Me*,[4] who analyzed answers from the Narcissistic Personality Inventory questionnaire used by psychologists to identify narcissism. No surprise, we parents are a big part of the problem, she says. Used to be, we all thought our kids were special *to us.* Now, we—along with a team of hired coaches—have decided our kids are special and the whole world should treat them accordingly.

Kids with narcissistic personality traits operate with an inflated sense of self, says Twenge. They're not clinically ill. But they think they're smarter than other people. They anticipate they'll be great workers, great spouses, or great parents. They are preoccupied with fantasies of unlimited success. They exaggerate their achievements, believe they're unique, and expect excessive praise. They're not confident, they're overconfident.

Narcissism, if you ask me, sounds awesome. And there are some short-term benefits, says Twenge. It feels good to think so highly of yourself. And some kids with narcissistic personality traits do better in public performances, such as acting, baseball pitching, skating, or singing—the exact disciplines in which our kids are being trained. But despite its perception, narcissism leads to more failures in life than it does victories, says Twenge. Our deeply held cultural belief that self-confidence creates success is wrong, she says. Success is achieved with hard work and self-control. Nothing more. Achievements build self-esteem, she says, not the other way around.

Social relationships will also advance both professional and personal goals. In fact, psychologists who know a few things about human happiness agree the biggest predictor of a person's happiness is the number and quality of friendships he or she has. As for professional success, it would be impossible to count the number of seminars and books devoted to networking.

Narcissists, however, drive people away. They lack empathy and don't care much about anyone else's good news. That makes it difficult to offer congratulations or appear interested in the lives of friends and associates. On top of that, narcissistic kids are often envious and bad at hiding it. The combination is relationship repellent. Always needing attention, they'll shove their way to the front of the class or the middle of photos; they're less than humble about wins and exaggerative when they're the recipients of compliments or achievements more modest kids wouldn't even bother to mention. Narcissistic kids may discover a friend has stopped calling or has decided to put more energy into someone else. They may be hit with a few nasty comments because, let's face it, if you walk around convinced you're unique and special, someone's gonna want to take you down a notch. No matter. The narcissist will decide those people are jealous. Or mean. She'll blame them, never herself.

When you're young, says Twenge, this is not the end of the world. Graduations bring fresh schools and new surroundings, while opportunities are fluid. New friends, relationships, or jobs are right around the corner. It's as young and older adults that those with narcissistic personality traits become depressed. While they're good at making friends, they're bad at keeping them. Their accomplishments won't likely fill any voids. Remember that we, their parents, set some pretty high standards. They're *stars* for God's sake, with exceptional talent and unstoppable potential. So yes, unless entire stadiums full of people are applauding, these kids will feel as though they haven't lived up to expectations. That's a recipe for unhappiness and disappointment. It's difficult to be satisfied with life, says Twenge.

Raise Them Better for Less

No one is suggesting we remove sports or drama from our kids' schedules. There are countless physical, intellectual, and psychological benefits to introducing our kids to all extracurricular activities. But when it comes to encouraging their success in these arenas, the most effective methods are either free or inexpensive.

Between the ages of three and eight years old, we can forget about private lessons, says Dr. Wurm. It's great to introduce singing, piano, baseball, acting, tennis, and soccer—heck, bring it all on—to learn what the kid likes. But it's very difficult for kids this little to pick up new skills. They'll work and work and work for months to learn things that will at later ages take just moments to master.

Instead, at this age, the best predictor of our children's success in a particular discipline is her love of and enjoyment in what she's doing, says Dr. Wurm. She asks: What sounds more loving and more enjoyable: (a) a child spending an hour alone with an adult stranger who is paid to drill in skills, or (b) receiving positive attention from parents and supportive social energy from friends while playing on a team? If you said *b,* Dr. Wurm agrees. We can enroll our kids in a low-priced community league or theater organization and also supplement after season or on the side with activities during which we bestow praise for hard work (meaning we have to pay attention). We as parents have been sold on the idea that someone else knows how to work with our kids better than we do, says Dr. Wurm. But we know these kids better than anyone! We can tell when they're trying hard and when they're only acting as if they're trying hard. We can call them out. A private teacher will not. And let's also remember, plenty of nonexperts have coached their kids to professional greatness, such as the parents of Venus and Serena Williams, for example. We can handle this.

"Your child's success in her extracurricular field—not to mention throughout life—will depend on her desire to challenge herself," says Dr. Wurm. "You can fuel that desire by rewarding her efforts. You want the child to tolerate frustration. You can cultivate her ability to do so by praising her endurance. It's that simple. And it's that cheap." For some, however, it's not that easy. To most of us, the idea of cheering the attempt, not the success, sounds lovely. But for a few of us accustomed to keeping score, it's pretty darn hard, says Dr. Wurm. As we tell our kids: Restraint today can be very gratifying tomorrow. And that applies here.

We should also work on organizing group activities, which should offer lots of cheering opportunities. We can invite kids to the park for soccer drills and cheer for the kids running like crazy. We can host softball games, and when a kid swings the bat with such concentration we can practically feel the focus, we'll pretend not to notice if she misses. Even for theater kids, we can call up karaoke videos on YouTube and clap for the children who are off-key but perform with the passion of a rock star. (Record video of it with your camera, while you're at it.) And there are plenty of cheap performance places. Community productions offer great exposure and training. And so do religious organizations, such as church or synagogue. That's where some of the best vocalists of all time—Whitney Houston, Jackie Mason (who was a synagogue cantor), Kevin Costner (who did musicals), Dudley Moore (who went to Magdalen College on an organ scholarship), Tina Turner, Aretha Franklin, and Lou Rawls[5]—all got their starts. They not only trained in front of an encouraging audience, but also got the kind of instruction that comes from imitating older and more experienced performers.

Kids about nine years old and older can begin to benefit from private lessons, says Dr. Wurm. But we can still cut costs in half or even by 75 percent. First, we probably do not need the highest-priced coach. Former national stars and Broadway-trained vocalists are more expensive. But college kids are often just as qualified. Private lessons can provide one-on-one, enriching instruction, but when you consider the end game—a local production of *The Little Mermaid?* The University Park Community finals?—our kids probably don't need to be the sole pupil in the room for an hour. We can get our children professional training for 50 percent less money by teaming up with one other student. Remember, practice, not instruction alone, is what cements the new skills. That's what makes routine. The only way to ensure these lessons are truly worth our money is to make sure our kids review the material afterward—over and over again. Using the same allotted time slot to review and rehearse can mean each lesson is more ingrained in our kids' minds. Practice is free.

Sure, it's pretty frustrating, too, reminding them to practice. So we threaten them, vowing to stop doing their laundry until they practice. But more effective than the fear of smelly socks—assuming your kids would even notice such a thing—is for us to build up our kids' willpower. That's what will drive them to practice more, concentrate harder, and truly become better performers.

Willpower—what some call self-control—will not only further their progress in whatever it is they're practicing today but also can help with achievements throughout their lives, says John Tierney, who with Florida State University professor Roy F. Baumeister, wrote *Willpower: Rediscovering the Greatest Human Strength*. This team proved that people with willpower not only perform better in sports and in school, but as they grow, those with the most self-control are also healthier, make more money, and are happier.

If you're having trouble fighting the flashback to the time your kid managed to sneak three more Kit Kat bars after you'd already put away the bag, don't worry. Willpower is like a muscle that we can all build up over time, says Tierney. There are very simple exercises and tips we can do with our kids. It's beneficial whether they're in sports or the arts or not, and for ourselves as well.

Strengthening your willpower requires simple (and free— remember we're still saving money) exercises our kids can incorporate into their regular routines. Sitting up straight at the table, making the bed every morning, brushing their teeth with their weaker hand, meditating, speaking in complete sentences, abolishing the word *like* from conversations, and not using contractions are all simple actions that force our kids to periodically concentrate when they might other- wise be operating on autopilot. Increased focus in these areas will spill over, says Tierney. Lab subjects, for example, were asked to perform activities requiring willpower, such as unsolvable puzzles, and then had them work on their posture at home. When they returned to the lab, they were more persistent in the activities. Tierney also points to Australian researchers who helped subjects better manage their money by crafting budgets. As the subjects sharpened their financial skills, they also ate healthier and kept their houses cleaner. "If you want to increase your willpower, make one simple change," says Tierney. "Building up self-control for one thing will build it up for anything else." It's never too early to start. The Ferber method—which involves letting kids cry until they teach themselves to sleep—is actually a will-power-building exercise, says Tierney. Religious people tend to have more self-control because attending services, praying, and fasting all require discipline.

When kids need willpower to achieve certain goals—running faster, losing weight, learning music—we can help support self-control, says Tierney. First, we have to help them clearly define the objective. Monitor their progress by keeping a chart showing the time spent and the improvements made, and reward them later. Like muscles, willpower can be fueled by food. In some studies, kids who ate breakfast behaved and performed better in school.

Willpower can also get depleted. Resisting the urge to text friends instead of studying uses up self-control, but decision making also pulls from those reserves. Expect your kids to have less willpower on days they've chosen electives or argued with a friend.

Rock-Solid Money Move

Bad news: Our income can disappear overnight. Companies have lay-offs. People get fired. Business owners lose huge accounts. Markets evaporate. Crooks steal. Products become obsolete. Mergers collapse. And you know what? Sometimes big earners—accountants, lawyers, engineers, product developers—quit their jobs in order to start businesses that can potentially reap big rewards later. But we can't even support those dreams unless we first have money set aside to support our families.

We must start emergency accounts that can protect our families in the face of the unexpected or even the planned disruption of our incomes. If things look bright today, then setting aside these funds should be a piece of cake. If your financial situation is perilous, then this exercise is even more critical, regardless of the current cuts you'll have to make.

However the dark days arrive, they sure can last a while. In 2010, economists told us the country's recessionary stats were in the rearview mirror. But there were still 14.8 million people unemployed—meaning they were actively looking but couldn't find jobs—according to the Bureau of Labor Statistics. When the bureau's economists took that count, 60 percent of those people had already been out of work for more than fifteen weeks while 43.3 percent of them hadn't had a paycheck in more than twenty-seven weeks, or more than six months. The government doesn't track unemployment for longer durations. (Or, for that matter, the number of parents who wind up kicking themselves for having in years past paid a private baseball or singing coach instead of saving money.) But it does count how many people leave the labor force—meaning they never got jobs but gave up trying—and in 2010 more than two million people threw their hands up and decided employment just wasn't happening.

Our emergency funds need to amount to enough money so we can all survive for a year without income. To find this amount you must do the following:

1. Go through your bills and list every expense, all year long. Some monthly expenses might include housing (mortgage or rental), car payments, utilities, cell phones, funding of college savings accounts, and cable television. Weekly expenses would include food, gas, entertainment, and private coaching. Don't forget annual tuitions.

2. From those, list the critical expenses you cannot survive without paying. Those will be housing, shelter, food, and medical care. And add them up for the year.

3. Then add in an additional $5,000 for emergencies. Cars have been known to break down at insensitive times. Roofs and home heaters are just as inconsiderate. We must budget for those.

4. Open a savings account—one that's FDIC insured—and start filling it as fast as you can until you reach the total.

5. Take a look at the original list of expenses. The ones that go unfunded are the ones you can live without during an income drought. Perhaps when it comes to private lessons, we'll have a different perspective on the term *emergency*.

CHAPTER SIX

Food

choose
FRESH
OVER FORMALDEHYDE

Save Estimated $30,274

The Stuff You'll Skip

These are estimates of what we might save by replacing 100 percent of our organic purchases with nonorganic items, which at this moment may not appeal, but perhaps after reading these costs and the following information, you'll decide to forgo a sizeable percentage of your organic consumption.

Meat: $40,875

Eggs: $2,020

Dairy: $10,173

Fruits and vegetables: $18,139

Nonorganic vs. Organic Food Spending Comparison

	Average per year of non-organic items	Total of 18 years (includes 3% inflation)
Cereals	$281	$7,055
Meat	$1,237	$31,130
Eggs	$74	$1,839
Dairy	$615	$15,446
Fruits and Vegetables	$1,066	$26,773

These are some very rough estimates on how much more organics cost over time. Guess what? **They're low.** These estimates were based on the spending of average Americans earning $88,828 a year for families of four people. The more you make, the more you spend. What's more, these are average. If you buy more vegetables or milk than the average American, your expenses are higher. The table below shows the calculations.*

Total Estimated Savings after 18 years: $30,274

Average per year of organic versions	Total over 18 years (includes 3% inflation)	Difference*
$281 (same)	$7,055	$0
$2,783	$72,005	$40,875
$154	$3,859	$2,020
$1,020	$25,619	$10,173
$1,790	$44,912	$18,139

L ydia is scared of cancer. None of us wants to take on that beast. But rarely does it haunt our every day, because not all of us have seen it up close, as Lydia did, when she was just eighteen years old and it beat the hell out of her younger brother.

Today with her own son to look after, Lydia buys organic and chemical-free everything, from baby wipes to eggs to her kids' mattresses, which the company claimed were chemical-free and certified by a special organization. Were they worth the $4,000 price tag?

Not likely.

Clean eating and chemical-free sleeping are worthy goals. The warnings are undeniable: Pesticides sprayed on fruit will alter hormone production and can cause cancer. And the mattresses we sleep on can emit VOCs (volatile organic chemicals) that can have adverse health effects, including central nervous system damage.

That's a miniature discussion of the issue. But you don't need much more to understand why parents will spend any amount of money at any time on any product that they believe will safeguard their families. We're protecting our kids from the synthetic dangers sprayed on and found inside what's put on the market by profit-centric, quality-indifferent corporate America.

The organics market has boomed into a $35 billion industry.[1] This works well for everyone. With organic products prevalent—even today on the shelves of Walmart and Costco—we don't have to drive to a country farmhouse for milk free of antibiotics.

The problem is that when it comes to shaping our perceptions, companies can be contortionists. And that includes those producing products that are seemingly on our side. EcoBaby Organics, Inc., may sound like a cuddly haven of capitalism. But US government lawyers would likely not agree. EcoBaby Organics sold mattresses it claimed were chemical-free, formaldehyde-free, and VOC-free. If that's not enough to push a natural parent to reach for her credit card, these mattresses were certified by an independent third party, an organization called the National Association of Organic Mattress Industry.

Nothing ruins a good chemical-free claim like actual testing. And EcoBaby had never done any, says the Federal Trade Commission.[2] What's more, the independent third party was actually an alter ego of the mattress company, meaning it wasn't independent or third. A party, however, was most certainly underway.

As parents, the desire to keep poisons away from our children and destruction away from our planet can cause us to needlessly overspend in ways that can actually harm our families. For starters, you can rid your mattress of many VOCs by simply airing it out in the yard. And, experts say, we can buy clean food and other products from local producers. Those growers or manufacturers are there and available to answer questions about pesticides—they're in organic foods too, you know—and farming methods, animal feeding, and product production. Shop at farmers' markets and local shops. Once you're in a supermarket, you're left interpreting labels. It's hard to look at a package making green promises and know who's actually speaking to us. Considering the various labels and certifications, it's often just as difficult to figure out what in God's name they're trying to say. Learn what these labels mean because, in some cases, you're spending more green in dollars than you're getting back in practices.

NATURAL

The word natural means "caused by nature," unless it happens to be stamped on a cereal box, ketchup bottle, or a personal care product, in which case it means absolutely nothing. There are no rules for using the word natural unless you're talking about meat, poultry, and egg products.[3] If someone's going to call those items "natural," they have to be minimally processed and contain no artificial ingredients. If you don't spend too much time wondering about the definition of *minimally* or *artificial* (seeing as the word *natural* requires no standards), you can concentrate instead on comparing the quality and prices for the things you buy, rather than relying on empty promises in the name.

ORGANIC

Most doctors and many consumer groups will tell us that money spent on organic food is well spent. But a peek behind the scenes at regulations and testing proves there's also a range of pesticide and even antibiotic residue found in products within the organic section. And, while the USDA standards on the Organic seal apply to agricultural products, you can call your company whatever you please. That means someone could open The Healthy Organic Delicious Nutritious Great for Kids Candy Corporation and—quite legally—sell processed sugar colored with Red Dye #40, so long as the packaging is not labeled *organic*. When shopping, we must be sure not to confuse company names with federal standards.

To wear the USDA Organic label, food must meet strict criteria. Processed food has to contain 95 percent organic ingredients, and if a food producer wants to tout even one organic ingredient, the other 70 percent of the package—at least—has to be organic, too[4]. Crops must be grown on land that's been free of synthetic substances for more than three years to wear the label. But that doesn't mean your produce will be entirely free of synthetic pesticides. That's because the EPA allows for accidents. The government is very well aware that organic and nonorganic farms share land. So, if testing finds some synthetic chemicals on organics, but at levels of less than 5 percent of what the EPA says is safe, well, that doesn't really count, does it?[5] Just as broken cookies have no calories.

A recent USDA pilot study, in an attempt to examine the testing requirements, looked at 327 samples of organic apples, strawberries, potatoes, bell peppers, and broccoli. A bit more than half of that organic produce (57.3 percent) had no detectable levels of synthetic pesticides. But the rest (42.7 percent) did have some synthetic residue. Of that bunch, 21 percent had levels greater than the EPA tolerance levels and were in violation of the organic regulations.

What's more, organic produce is not produced without pesticides; it's produced without synthetic pesticides. That sounds perfectly reasonable until you meet Jeff Gillman, a horticulturist who authored five books including *The Truth About Organic Gardening*. Gillman assures us that natural poison can be perfectly toxic to humans, pointing to snake venom as a good example of a substance that even we amateur naturalists would agree isn't man-made but is certainly not welcome in our bloodstreams. The same can be said about many of the insecticides that are produced naturally by plants and have been cleared under the USDA's organic standards, says Gillman.

Natural pesticides are less effective, says Gillman, but that doesn't make them less harmful. In his book, Gillman points to research done by Joseph Kovach in apple orchards proving that natural pesticides are more frequently reapplied because they are less potent. The environmental consequences, at least, can be greater than a single application of a synthetic pesticide. Gillman says that when it comes to toxicity, we have to consider the dosage. Many substances can be poisonous at high levels and almost anything can be safe at low levels.

But we'll likely never learn how much of a natural pesticide resides on organic produce because no one is testing that. Each state-run program certifying farms is required to test at least 5 percent of the agricultural businesses in its jurisdiction, but only for prohibited substances—synthetic pesticides, arsenic, and antibiotics.

If that agency believes there is a local violator, it is certainly welcome to go out and bring the fruit or vegetables to an official lab. But it must also be willing to pay for these efforts. If you're familiar with the financial generosity of state-run programs, you may aim low when forecasting the amount of testing that's likely to occur under this part of the plan.

This isn't to discourage you from buying organic fruits and vegetables. It's merely to prevent any of us—but mostly my friend Lydia—from experiencing severe panic at the thought of buying and consuming nonorganic produce. Moving from organic to nonorganic produce is not the automatic equivalent of moving from good to evil.

Yes, those extremes—squeaky-clean and pesticide-soaked—are perhaps lining some shelves. But ask researchers from Cornell who reviewed organic practices and they'll tell you that all organic produce is not farmed equally.[6] When it comes to the amount of pesticide and antibiotic residue to be found, there is a huge variation in crops, even across organic farms. Produce from some organic farms will have a lot of pesticide residue; produce from other organic farms will have much less. That's true, too, for nonorganic produce: There's a range in levels of residue even across farms operating as nonorganic. It's difficult to imagine the health professional who would suggest we spend our produce budgets on less—but yet organic—produce. Perhaps even your own doctor would recommend two fat boxes of nonorganic strawberries— translating to fruit each day—over one small box of organic berries. Even the Environmental Working Group—a watchdog for human and eco safety—says the health benefits of a diet rich in fruits and vegetables outweigh risks of pesticide exposure.

Some researchers, including those at Washington State University's Center for Sustaining Agriculture and Natural Resources[7]—will say organic foods are more nutritious, containing more antioxidants. But Stanford University researchers looked at 223 comparisons of nonorganic and organic fruits, vegetables, grains, meats, poultry, milk, and eggs, and combed though studies that examined either pesticides, nutrition, antibiotic resistance, and food-borne pathogens.[8] They managed to look at how the foods affected thirteen thousand organic and nonorganic eaters. Those included pregnant women, children, and nonpregnant adults. Organic-eating children had lower pesticide levels in their urine. They didn't find a comparable test for adults. But grown-up organic eaters didn't have more fatty acids in their breast milk than the nonorganic eaters. Their semen and urine was the same when it came to plasma, vitamin content, antioxidant activity, or ability to protect against DNA damage. And neither group—not the organic or nonorganic consumers—had any more eczema or wheezing.

They could not determine that organic produce was more nutritious, except to say some varieties had more phosphorus. But seeing as the only factor contributing to a phosphorus deficiency is near starvation, the researchers didn't consider this particularly significant. Both organic and nonorganic animal products were commonly contaminated with salmonella and campylobacter, though one study showed organic produce to have a higher risk for being contaminated with *E. coli*. Using manure as fertilizer can do that to a crop.

Ah yes, manure. When it's collected from nonorganically raised animals—who, when raised in close quarters, are frequently treated for infections—the manure can also deposit antibiotics into soil. Scientists at the University of Minnesota, who were funded by the USDA, looked at three food crops—corn, lettuce, and potatoes—grown in both organic and nonorganic farms on soil treated with hog manure containing sulfamethazine.[9] That veterinary drug, commonly used to treat bacterial diseases in humans and animals and to promote growth in cattle, sheep, pigs, and poultry, was taken up by all three crops. The more medicine found in the manure, the more that was found in the plants. The scientists said in their report that root crops—such as potatoes, carrots, and radishes—that directly come in contact with soil may be particularly vulnerable to antibiotic contamination.

ORGANIC OR SUSTAINABLE FISH

These designations are titles your supermarket's fishing crew assigned to its own products, with its own conviction. There are no federal regulations that make fish or shellfish sustainable or organic. There are no tests for toxicity. There are no standards to follow. There are, however, higher prices.

NON-GMO

GMOs (genetically modified organisms) are crops that have been manipulated by scientists, who alter the genes so the plants can better resist disease or tolerate pesticides. There are only eight crops in the United States with a GMO version: soybeans, corn, papaya, canola, cotton, alfalfa, sugar beets, and summer squash. Organic foods cannot contain GMOs.[10] But foods stamped as "Non-GMO" are not automatically organic.

That means products stamped "non-GMO" are can be produced with herbicides and pesticides. They may come from an operation that confines its animals. And sometimes products wearing this stamp wouldn't typically be made with a GMO crop anyway. It could be more difficult to make organic coconut nectar with soybeans or papaya than it is to keep it free of genetically modified organisms.

FAIR TRADE

When it comes to buying food labeled "Fair Trade," you should expect that at least one product ingredient was produced in a factory or farm practicing workplace safety, paying reasonable wages, and prohibitive of child labor. When you consider the widespread reports of slavery on cocoa bean farms or reckless use of knives in slaughterhouses, Fair Trade practices are worthy of our financial support.

Fair Trade USA (www.fairtradeusa.org) is the organization affiliated with the USDA, but because there are several authoritative organizations willing to issue Fair Trade labels,[11] it could be difficult to know exactly how much of a product has been manufactured under the conditions you're hoping to support. For example, you may read ice cream is made with Fair Trade chocolate chips or Fair Trade vanilla. But often farms responsible for milk production for the ice cream—even right here in the United States—can have unsafe working conditions.

Because violators of those laws are rife in some notable industries—coffee, cocoa, chocolate, tea, and bananas, to name a few—even one Fair Trade ingredient can in some cases be very meaningful. But the goal should be for all companies in all countries to create and uphold safe, legal, and suitable working conditions. Not for us to feel good supporting these goals in some factories while at the same time turning a blind eye to others.

HUMANE
You'll have to take the company's word for it.

RECYCLABLE
This word means that the package can be separated from the trash and used again to make a new product. But just because humans have created the technology to reuse that material doesn't mean your community is using it.[12] Every community sets its own recycling rules.

Common unrecyclable materials include pizza boxes, paper towels and tissue, and plastic bags, though usually you can take those back to the retailer. You'll have to learn what's recycled in your local area. As a side note, some printer manufacturers will take back their cartridges.

BIODEGRADABLE AND OXODEGRADABLE
Oxodegradable means that an object will degrade when it comes in contact with oxygen, which makes it exactly the same as biodegradable. Neither is worth our extra money. All of our garbage is delivered directly to landfills, and those are required by law to be sealed to keep out sunlight, air, and moisture, so the garbage doesn't seep into the air and water supply.[13] Without air, nothing is degrading. Ever.

COMPOSTABLE
This helps you only if you have compost, which is a vat of trimmings from fruits, vegetables, and other products that we'd be accumulating to enrich soil. If contributing to community compost, you'd have to ask what's permitted. If you're not doing one of those things, then the "compostable" stamp helps no one.

BAMBOO FABRICS

Bamboo is famous for its amazing ability to grow quickly without pesticides. This is a miracle for those of us who demand pesticide-free flooring or furniture. But when you turn bamboo into fabric you do not create a clean and natural textile as many companies will claim. You create rayon. Regular, synthetic, rayon.[14] What's more, the chemicals used in the transformation are toxic. The process releases pollutants into the air. Even when bamboo is the plant source of your rayon clothing or sheets, absolutely none of the original properties are left behind.

TESTED GREEN

You don't have to worry about overpaying for products wearing this certification because it's no longer around. The government ordered the company of the same name to stop issuing the seals after determining they were meaningless, were available to anyone willing to pay the registration fee, and—despite the title—did not involve a single test.[15] It's nice to shop with a conscience but even better if you can Google a label to see if it's issued by a reputable organization.

CFC OR OZONE FRIENDLY

In 1978 chlorofluorocarbons (CFCs—chemical substances that can deplete the earth's protective ozone layer) were banned for use in aerosol products. But just because a product doesn't contain any CFCs doesn't mean it won't harm the earth's atmosphere. VOCs, found in household cleaning products such as floor polishes, charcoal lighter fluid, windshield wiper fluid, and hair spray also contribute to ground-level ozone.[16]

SPI SYMBOL

This symbol indicates the Society of the Plastics Industry, and while this would be an excellent name for the large group of women I know in Miami who have surgically pulled back all signs of aging on their faces, it's actually a trade association for workers in this line of manufacturing. It stamps numbers from 1 to 7 on plastics to classify the materials. Numbers 1 and 2 mean a container is more likely to be recyclable.

NANO SILVER

Silver has antimicrobial properties and has for centuries been used to fight bacteria without toxicity to humans and animals. So a company went ahead and engineered it into tiny particles that could be woven into clothing, blankets, and carpets. The idea was that the silver would suppress the growth of the microbes that cause odors, stains, and discoloration in workout wear. But the Natural Resource Defense Council wasn't impressed. The organization went ahead and sued the EPA, saying that wearing or eating these particles—which is how most babies enjoy their blankets—can penetrate organs and tissues in the body that larger forms of silver cannot reach, like the brain and lungs.[17] Today you can find it in food containers and nursing bras, but because there's been little testing, we might be better off saving our money and not finding it at all.

Green-Buyer Beware

The following products were forced by the government to stop making green claims. The lesson we can learn is not to believe everything we read. To help us all shop skeptically, here's a list of claims that really were too good to be true.

VOC-free paints: The Sherwin-Williams Company said its paints were VOC-free, but that was true only for the uncolored base paints, the government says. Once tinting was added—as changing the color of walls is the main reason people paint them—there were in fact VOCs.[18] The complaint was filed by a competitor, and Sherwin-Williams disputed the testing.

VOC-free mattresses: Talk about not sleeping alone, EcoBaby Organics had lots of company when making VOC-free bed claims. Relief-Mart said its Biogreen memory foam mattresses had no VOC off-gassing and lacked the odors commonly associated with memory foam mattresses. And Essentia Natural Memory Foam Company, Inc., said that not only did its mattresses lack VOCs, but also they were chemical-free and made from 100 percent natural materials. The FTC alleged neither could prove those claims[19] and they entered into an agreement barring the companies from making these claims without scientific evidence.

Diapers: Down to Earth Designs, Inc., told us it created a plastic-free diaper system. In addition to the reusable outer shell called gPants, we'd have to buy disposable inner liners called gRefills and baby wipes, called gWipes.[20] The company said the diapers are biodegradable—which the government alleged the company couldn't prove—and compostable. Even if that were true, you can only compost wet diapers—or those from the box without using them—seeing as you cannot compost human feces. (Compost, for those beginning farmers, is used to fertilize crops.)

Raise Them Better for Less

Organics and eco-friendly products are expensive, costing sometimes two or three times more than their nonorganic counterparts. You may be willing to pay any price to save your family and planet. But it's not guaranteed that you'll accomplish those worthy goals with every purchase.

Ever since big business helped itself to a share of these naturally friendly markets, the meaning behind each label is about as clear as the congressional legislation regulating it. The government's guidelines have evolved to ensure small-time farming customs can be carried out on very large scales. And it's easy to misinterpret the earth-friendly assurances. This doesn't mean we shouldn't support these causes. But we should think twice before sacrificing our own finances in exchange for maybes. Here are surefire ways to live clean while cutting costs:

GET A BROILER PAN

For $16, you can drain harmful dioxin from any meat—organic or not. Dioxin is very different from a synthetic pesticide. It's the name for a group of toxic chemicals that are created from processes such as burning waste and chemical manufacturing.[21] These gasses seep into the air, water, soil, and the organic and nonorganic food chain. They land on produce, and while we can wash them off, grazing farm animals typically do not. Instead cows, for example, eat the dioxin in their grass, they breathe it in the air, they drink it from water, and eventually they store it in their fat.

That's where we come in. Everyone knows cow fat is delicious.

But it's also easy to avoid on our plates. Rather than frying or stewing your steak (chicken or burgers too), slap your meat on a broiling pan and the fat automatically drips to the bottom during cooking. And because experts tell us dioxin is most frequently found in dairy products, switch to the nonfat varieties of milk, yogurt, and cottage cheese at no additional cost.

BUY ORGANIC ONLY WHEN IT COUNTS

Each year, the Environmental Working Group (ENG) tests nonorganic produce and then reports the varieties wearing the most and least pesticide residue. These lists are called the "Dirty Dozen" and the "Clean Fifteen," and for those of us who want to buy organic fruits and vegetables when it's necessary, these findings can govern our actions in the aisle.

At the moment, the dirtiest of the dozen includes grapes, for which a single sample contained fifteen pesticides. It also includes celery, cherry tomatoes, imported snap peas, and strawberries, which showed thirteen different pesticides each. More than 99 percent of apple samples and imported nectarine samples tested positive for at least one pesticide residue. The organic versions of these are good bets. Or you can on some occasions forget them completely.

There's plenty of nonorganically grown produce that's practically pesticide-free. During the last round of testing, some 89 percent of pineapples, 82 percent of kiwi, 80 percent of papayas, 88 percent of mangos, and 61 percent of cantaloupe had no residues, says the EWG. Only 1 percent of avocados showed any trace at all. You also have in this category cabbage, sweet peas, onions, and asparagus, all of which rarely test positive for pesticides, says the EWG.

Finally, check out the Dirty Dozen Plus, a category the watchdog created so it could warn us about organophosphate and carbamate insecticides. They're highly toxic and can, even in low doses, impair intelligence and brain development in children, according the EWG. Over the past two decades, organophosphates have been pulled from most produce but are still permitted on leafy greens such as kale and also hot peppers. The EWG suggests we buy organic varieties.

WASH YOUR PRODUCE

Jeff Gillman, the horticulturist who studies pesticides for a living, says he himself buys only nonorganic fruits and vegetables. He washes them with warm water. What's more, pesticides are reduced when produce is cooked, according to the Environmental Working Group's website.

CHOOSE FROZEN PRODUCE

Frozen produce frequently contains the most nutrients, which are locked in during the icing process that typically happens at or very near the farm. It's also much cheaper, even if it's organic. Pack in your freezer pounds of organic berries, broccoli, and spinach for

sometimes much less money than you'd spend even on the nonorganic stuff. You get more for your money, and that includes time—
one of the most valuable resources around.

VOTE

As an American, voting is your privilege, your responsibility, and also
your ticket to clean food. It also happens to be free, if you don't count
the fact that politicians are always asking for campaign contributions.
Those are the people who craft the laws dictating whether we're safe
or scared in the supermarket, and they can get those awesome law-
writing gigs only if we vote for them. We give them jobs as senators
or House representatives. Those two bodies make up Congress, and
that's where everything happens when it comes to your concerns about
pesticides, safety, inspection, and standards.

It's hard to keep up with it all, but Food Policy Action is a
group that was created by environmentalists and organic producers
wanting us to elect leaders who care about keeping food production
clean, plentiful, and environmentally safe. To that end, it counts
who votes for support and reports where each member stands on the
laws that protect those interests. Then it gives each one a score, so we
can decide for ourselves who exactly our reps are working for when
they're in that chamber.

EAT FROSTED CHOCOLATE TOASTER PASTRIES:

To be fair, that is an extremely loose interpretation of Dr. Wurm's
actual advice on the subject of food indulgences. But when discussing with her the matter of the markets being flooded with organic
versions of some sugar-filled and artificially flavored favorites such
as Pop-Tarts or Rice Krispies Treats, Dr. Wurm pointed out that
yes, perhaps organic toaster pastries will protect us from some artificial flavors and pesticides. But we shouldn't be feeding any of these
options to our kids so much that it makes a difference. "Just because
it's organic doesn't mean it's healthy or that it doesn't have too much

sugar," says Dr. Wurm. "Anything with added sugar is something that should be limited in your child's diet."

Take organic marshmallow treats. They contain a nice list of pronounceable ingredients. The marshmallows are made from organic brown rice syrup, organic cane sugar, organic guar gum, and sea salt. Still, to a body, that's sugar and salt. If we want to limit exposure to pesticides, we can sparingly give these to kids, says Dr. Wurm, but we have to treat them as indulgences.

Baking allows for indulgences and family time, for even less money and more nutrients. Dr. Wurm gets her recipes from ChopChopMag. org, which offers ideas for bananas, honey, pears, black cocoa, and dates. As a bonus, baking with your kids mean there's a good chance they'll put down their cell phones.

As for those frosted Pop-Tarts? I can accurately report at this juncture that Dr. Wurm does say that the occasional frosted, goo-filled pastry will not serve as the barrier between our children and excellent health. "What you don't want to be is crazy," says Dr. Wurm. "Restriction doesn't work with kids. Modeling good habits at home does." We have to let them eat what's served at birthday parties, even if that involves cotton candy. We can't forbid grandparents from pulling out the sugary supermarket cookies for our kids. They'll live.

TOSS YOUR MOISTURIZERS AND BABY LOTIONS:
We always thought our kids were cute enough to eat. So it's fitting Dr. Wurm suggests that when at home, we soothe their skin with oils from coconuts, almonds, avocados, and olives instead of highly manufactured, scented, unscented, or even natural moisturizers. The problem with most commercial products is that they contain parabens, which are preservatives used in creams and cosmetics to prevent growth of bacteria. If you find the idea of bacteria to be troubling, wait until you hear about parabens. They are endocrine disrupters, which are linked to breast cancer and reproductive cancers, says Dr. Wurm.

The chemicals in these creams can be even more dangerous than the kind found in food. That's because the saliva and the stomach has natural enzymes to help process whatever we stuff in our mouths, says Dr. Wurm. Our skin is also one big digestive organ, with our bodies absorbing whatever we slather on. But it's got no defense system.

Natural oils aren't just better, they're also cheaper. You can get sixteen ounces of olive oil for $4.97, compared to $9.19 for sixteen ounces of a very popular brand-name cream that I'm afraid to name. Plus the edible option goes further, because you'll use less each time you lather. Shop for them in the food section—not the cosmetics aisle—or you'll pay a premium.

You should still pack the regular stuff in your diaper bag, says Dr. Wurm. The natural stuff can be greasy and much less convenient. You want to keep your frustration level very, very low, otherwise you might decide to forget the whole idea.

BUY CHEAP SOAP

A plain soap such as Ivory comes without the key ingredient found in antibacterial soaps: a chemical called Triclosan, which has been found to alter hormone production in animals, says the NRDC.[22] It costs less—about $3.99 for ten bars compared to $10.99 for just three bars of its bacteria-fighting counterpart.

You might be better off. Studies that followed urban families—only half of which used antibacterial soap[23]—found that when it came to illnesses including cough, fever, diarrhea, and skin infections, there was no difference in the two groups. In fact, plain soap people could prove to be healthier in the long run, says Dr. Wurm. She says doctors are frequently tossing around something called the hygiene hypothesis, a theory that holds microbe exposure is good. Excessive cleanliness, on the other hand, disrupts normal development of the immune system and makes us prone to autoimmune diseases.

DRINK TAP WATER

It appears that select executives in the bottled water industry have managed to pull over on us one of the greatest and most successful marketing ploys of all time. You gotta hear this: They turned on tap water, filled up plastic bottles, and then slapped on labels with the words *purified* or *filtered*. By some estimates, 40 percent of all bottled water is drawn from the public water supply, according to a report from the Natural Resources Defense Council, which conducted a four-year study that involved one thousand samples of 103 types of bottled water plus an in-depth assessment of its sources, contamination problems, and governance.[24] Sometimes the tap water was treated with carbon filtration or ozonation, which we can do at home with a water filter. But sometimes, it was just plain tap water!

For the privilege of enjoying tap water served to us in environmentally impairing plastic bottles, we have been willing to pay a premium of between 240 percent and 10,000 percent per gallon. On the flip side, that's how much less it would cost us if we simply start turning on our own faucets and use our own cups. So let's do that, people. And use the savings to buy water filters if we're so worried about contaminants. Or BPA-free water bottles if we need convenience.

Because while the FDA has agreed to watch the industry more heavily since the NRDC study was conducted, one thing hasn't changed: Most tap water is perfectly safe. Public municipal water supplies are heavily regulated and required to perform periodic testing. They must even issue annual reports.

Buying It!

Still willing to pay a premium to protect the world? Great. For just pennies more each hour that you use your lights and television, residents almost everywhere can pay for green power.

You don't need a windmill. Your run-of-the mill utility provider may very well be able to sell you the kind of energy made from wind, the sun, and even piles of garbage. Garbage emits energy, you know. Good news: The earth is filled with garbage! It's rotting practically everywhere! We also happen to be in large supply of sun, wind, and manure—all of which never run out. But here's something you need to know: The premiums we'll have to pay are contributions to our communities, not our homes. Special green electrons do not come into your electric sockets or light switches. You get the same current as always. That's because power companies provide electricity to entire areas—including your home—using a giant power grid. These grids connect to countless transmission lines that are interconnected within neighborhoods and cities and even states. When you lose power, everyone loses power. We're all in this power circle together.

If you select, say, solar energy, your utility company in turn takes your money and spends it powering *the grid* using solar technology. The electrons generated from those solar efforts could wind up anywhere. You never know the color of the electricity that gets to your gate. It's still an effort worthwhile for your world and your wallet. For starters, renewable energy is often entirely clean. Every kilowatt-hour of renewable power saves us the emission of more than one pound of carbon dioxide— amounting to perhaps thousands of emissions each year.

Then consider this: The more people who choose renewable energy, the more economical it becomes. With many contributions to the same cost—solar power, wind turbines— everyone's share gets lower.

It's happening already. In the past two decades, green energy prices have fallen while conventional energy prices have risen. Very often, the two are in line. Even better: Some states offer tax credits and other financial incentives for residents who choose green energy. If green energy isn't available in your state, you may be able to spend extra money on other energy-saving methods in exchange for financial incentives. For example, in Colorado, homeowners who buy solar technology to heat their pools can get back 15 percent of the sales price to use on installation. San Diego, California, will waive the permit fee for solar projects.[25]

The Department of Energy lists the Green Power options in your state, provided at http://apps3.eere.energy.gov/green-power/markets/pricing.shtml?page=1. Here's what you need to know about green power lingo. Those "premium" prices are listed in cents, not dollars. That means 2.25¢ translates to two and a quarter pennies. Not $2.25. And 0.3 means one-third of a penny. Translation: You'd need to use three hours of electricity before the premium amounted to 1¢.

PV stands for *photovoltaic*, which is the process of converting sunlight to electricity. Works on everything from watches to air conditioning to electric fences.

Wind turbines are the cheapest form of green energy. Wind moves the blades of an energy-producing machine. Problem is, wind isn't always around when you need it (only when your hair looks really good).

Methane is rubbish, quite literally. The piles of garbage stinking away in landfills produce methane, which can be used to produce electricity.

Digester gas is made from wastewater. The gas is produced quickly in airtight containers. Based on the fumes emitted from Tupperware containers rescued from the back of my fridge, I know this is true.

Rather than throw away perfectly good cow manure, energy experts have found it more efficient to pull out the methane and use it as energy.

Rock-Solid Money Move

All of us—even those on strict organic diets—are going to die. Hopefully that won't happen for decades and decades and decades *and decades* from now. But that's not guaranteed either. We need to at this very moment, while we're feeling great, put down on paper specific directives for others on exactly how to raise our children and how to spend our money in the unlikely event we're not around.

Don't think of estate planning as a contract with death. Instead, consider each document your ticket to immortality. These papers carry out the strategies you set for your kids if you're not around. And they're legal documents, meaning everyone must follow your instructions—*even your mother-in-law.*

In lieu of your directives, you'll leave behind a disaster. If you think arguments over holiday pies can get heated, wait until you see what happens when there's life insurance money at stake and custody battles to be had. It's not just emotional warfare for your kids; it's also financial. These disagreements spark the kind of court fights that can rip right though the life insurance money you left them. And you *still* won't get your say.

I sat down with Israel Sands, an attorney in Miami specializing in estate planning. And he shared the four estate documents our lawyers must help us draft today so we can live knowing our kid's well-being is protected well beyond tomorrow.

A TRUST

If you think that's just for rich kids, then it's important to remember this: That's exactly what yours will become after cashing the life insurance check—it should be enough money to support them for many years. This is a very good thing, as living and education expenses are enormous. However, an eighteen-year-old with access to a bounty big enough to fund college—but without the legal requirements of having to spend it there—is a recipe for a Ferrari and a summer's worth of nightclubbing. "You need to protect your children from the assets so it doesn't cut off their incentive to make something of themselves," says Sands.

A trust is a document that exists to administer wealth, says Sands. Your child is the beneficiary—he or she will *benefit* from the trust. You are the trust creator and, while you're alive, the trustee. You'll name a successor trustee in the event you're not around.

Pick this person carefully. The successor trustee has a critically important financial job having nothing to do with love or affection, so good news: It doesn't have to be the same person getting custody of your kids. Pick someone responsible, honest, and financially savvy. This person should be wise when hiring an investment advisor, because this money will wait for your kids in the financial markets. The successor trustee cannot benefit personally from the funds, though some states allow this person to collect a fee.

The successor trustee will also distribute this money to your kids for their education, health, and maintenance. But you'll have to decide how frequently to administer funds. Some people use increments (for example, one-third at age twenty-one, one-third at age thirty-one and one-third at age forty-one). But more recently, parents have decided to protect those assets by storing them in the trust and paying expenses directly from there—everything from rent to tuition to supermarket purchases, the food-buying done though gift cards. "If your money is in a trust, you have no absolute right to it," says Sands. "These assets are forever protected from your creditors, your predators, and your future ex-spouses." Trusts keep the assets protected from lawsuits, if your kid should accidentally hurt someone or, say, marry the wrong person.

This is also an excellent place to list your priorities and values, says Sands. You might tell your kids to take an annual family vacation. You might weave in personal stories about hard work and achievement. You might reserve money for religious ceremonies.

Before meeting your lawyer—who will no doubt charge you by

the hour—know whom you will appoint as successor trustee. Don't make that one of your children, says Sands, as that's the best way to destroy a relationship between siblings.

LAST WILL AND TESTAMENT

If you have a spouse, that person automatically gets your money and your kids. (This is my personal motivation for staying alive, as my own husband is genetically incapable of packing a suitcase for two girls or purchasing feminine supplies.) After that, you'll divvy up your stuff, but most of your assets will just pour over into the trust.

As for who gets your kids in the event that you're single or you and your spouse both pass away? That's the hard part (I'm working to stay alive for this reason as well), as you'll have to pick your kid some new parents. You'll name the guardian—and in the event that person is not available, a successor guardian. Think about who shares your values. Think about who can create a nurturing home. Think about who will agree to the job. Because you can't leave your kids to, say, Brad Pitt and Angelina Jolie or Bill and Melinda Gates. This is one of those processes that you'll find easy to put off for weeks and months and years. Don't. Without your instructions and the potential guardian's agreement, a judge decides the fate of your family. That judge could see things very differently than you—possibly even viewing your parents as *sane*.

Your will also contains your burial instructions. Consider completing them on a separate, pull-apart page, says Sands. That way, your personal representative—you'll have to pick that person, too—can simply hand the page to the funeral director, who won't be privy to all your personal financial information.

There's another person you have to pick and, at this point, it seems I'd better start being nicer to my relatives. That's because we'll all need someone to have power of attorney, a person who will act as though they are you in the event you are incapacitated. They'll pay your bills or sue your neighbor if necessary.

And finally, we have to leave behind health care directives. Do we want to be on life support? Should a doctor force-feed us? And are there any circumstances under which someone may take us to Oregon, where we can live for six months before participating in doctor-assisted suicide? If these options seem horrible, think about how your kids will view them. When we take control, they won't have to feel guilty. And we don't want to waste perfectly good guilt when we can't even delight in the results.

Your Dream Team

Hopefully you'll never need these people to carry out your wishes. But in the event you die, you'll need a lot of people to help your kids live on. Your dream team will be made up of the following:

A trustee: to invest and administer your life insurance money.

A personal representative: to execute your will.

Guardians for your kid: to take custody if you're not around.

Power of attorney: you'll give this to the person who will act on your behalf if you're incapacitated.

CHAPTER SEVEN

Medical Care

choose
GOOD HEALTH
OVER HEARSAY

Save Estimated $6,421.87

The Stuff You'll Skip

An initial consultation with a healer who does not take health insurance can cost anywhere from $80 to $250, and the follow-up appointments—and you can be sure there will be follow-up appointments—will be the same or less.

Testing, say, for food sensitivities/genetics/neurotransmitters/blood type can cost $850 or more. Then you'll need supplements/nutriceuticals/homeopathic tablets made from—at least in my case—diluted duck livers.

Total Cash Outlay: $1,900
Total Invested Savings after 18 Years: $6,421.87

There's nothing alarming about a four-year-old having eczema. Unless of course the US Food and Drug Administration links the steroid cream you've been applying to the kid's eczema—almost nightly—to lymphoma. And in the same breath advises doctors to prescribe it with caution, and even then, only for short-term use.

So, um, then can I panic?

Don't bother answering. (I panicked.) And since everyone knows it's silly to waste a perfectly good state of wild hysteria on otherwise rational thinking, I instead lost faith in drug makers and the doctors who seemed so willing to help line their pockets. I turned to a homeopath employing a practice from the 1700s but charging rates not covered by modern insurance companies. It cost me over $1,400 for food sensitivity tests, a homeopathic consultation, and two work-ups and medicine.

The only money-saving news is that my health insurance did agree to pay the $5,000 hospital bill years later after my daughter—thanks to open and uncured eczema—contracted a pretty serious case of impetigo. And had to be hooked up to an IV of antibiotics for forty-eight hours. The rash on her arms, according to the emergency room physician, looked angry. She had a fever.

I don't discount homeopathy—which involves a system of natural and highly diluted remedies to help the body cure itself—as trusted parents and professionals swear it works. And still, like most parents, I prefer to handle things naturally. I'd rather *not* give my kids antibiotics or steroids if honey or coconut oil will do the trick.

I'm not alone. Many of us raising children today were ourselves kids in an era of overprescribed antibiotics, when physicians told pregnant women to continue smoking cigarettes for weight control.

Now as adults we hear stories about health care providers who overtest and overmedicate. (If you happen to be a doctor, we *also* hear stories about parents absolutely and often irrationally demanding extra tests and medication.) And we all together witnessed in 2008 the makers of children's cough medicine suddenly change their minds and their labels to essentially say, *Know what? Turns out you better not give this stuff to kids under four years old.* We are a new generation of parents and we want a gentler, safer way to cure our kids. Everyone knows nature can produce healing properties. What's better for a cold than vitamin C? And for this, we are willing to leave our health plans behind and pay out of pocket for services and remedies that are not covered by insurance companies.

We are so worried about the side effects of synthetic medicines—which ironically contain ingredients that actually *have* been tested and proven to work—that we are willing to pay healers who claim to have picked ingredients from the ground. We know how to be skeptical of drug makers and *their* products. But we give the natural people a pass. We want so badly to believe that we can get the results our kids need, risk-free, that we often skip the part about asking for scientific research and we take down our guard and pull out our wallets, spending $33 billion on complementary and alternative medicine in 2007, says the National Institutes of Health. Of our money, $14.8 billion went toward natural products—not counting vitamins—and $11.9 billion went toward an estimated 354.2 million visits to practitioners such as acupuncturists, chiropractors, massage therapists, and homeopaths, says NIH.

Western medicine, which typically involves evidence-based decisions made by people with medical degrees, is totally on board, in some cases making big commitments to natural therapies. The NIH—our government's primary agency for health research—has set up the National Center for Complementary and Alternative Medicine (NCCAM). And the teaching hospital of Harvard University, Boston Children's Hospital, has an integrative therapies team to provide a holistic approach to patients. Its website says the team promotes Reiki, a practice that provides healing energy through touch. The bottom line here is that Ivy League doctors are practicing an ancient Japanese therapy involving unseen life force energies. This is huge.

But, when it comes to many of the products sold in stores, some of the natural implications can be misleading. It's easy for us to read some of the labels and believe that what's inside the boxes are derived from ingredients that are wholesome and pure within the earth: Things we can consume in unlimited quantities, like sunlight. Things created by God or the Universe or the Deity—whatever force you happen to believe creates things. The problem is that no one, and no agency, is regulating natural and alternative supplements and services. Sometimes, the only commonality between God's work and many natural products is that government isn't watching the creation of either one. The FDA regulates the herbs and natural remedies on store shelves as dietary supplements,[1] meaning, more specifically, they're completely unregulated. There is no approval process. Supplements are not tested for safety. They are not tested for effectiveness. They are *not even tested for confirmation that the ingredients on the label are actually the ingredients in the product.* That's the job of the manufacturers making the stuff. They're supposed to watch themselves. This leaves a gap between what's proven to work and what's being sold to us. This space is wide, meaning there's lots of room for us to get ripped off—even hurt—simply trying to heal our children safely.

At this point it's worth repeating before anyone starts screaming (by "anyone" I mean Dr. Gwen Wurm, the vegetarian pediatrician who wrote the forward for this book) that natural remedies are awesome. *We love and prefer natural remedies!* But even our meat-free doctor warns that much of the expensive stuff out there—at best—doesn't do anything. And at worst, and in rare cases, it can cost our kids their good health. "Just because a supplement is all natural does not automatically mean it's safe," says Dr. Wurm. Sometimes these supplements cause direct harm. Other times the result is letting ill-nesses go untreated, like my daughter's eczema.

Remember that cyanide is one of Mother Earth's wonderful bounties. Arsenic too. Even the FDA says that homeopathic treatments—such as those containing heavy metals like mercury or iron—can cause unfavorable and sometimes serious adverse affects.[2] Here, let's travel though some of the less productive stops on a tour of the natural medicine market:

Coughs and Colds

We've all felt our own chests hurt when watching our kids cough. We worry when they can't breathe. And we're all tired when they can't sleep. Doctors won't of course prescribe antibiotics for viral illnesses. So the natural medicine market has beefed up its offerings in this area.

The American Academy of Pediatrics, meanwhile, recommends a nighttime dose of soothing buckwheat honey for kids who are coughing and over twelve months old.[3] About 1/2 teaspoon to 1 teaspoon as needed, which in layman's terms means we can give lots of honey. Pour it on. One study—published in the academy's journal—found that three varieties of honey including eucalyptus, citrus, or labiatae can reduce the frequency and severity of coughing. Honey helps both kids and parents sleep better.

This, not incidentally, points out Dr. Wurm, is exactly the kind of natural medicine that Western doctors can get behind. Because it's been tested. In studies. On children. It also happens to be the kind of science that companies can package, market, and sell. One brand of children's remedies boasts that its honey cough syrup contains just three ingredients: water, honey, and a preservative. But if not for that darn preservative, a person with even limited culinary talents could perhaps whip up a batch of this elixir at home. You know, with water and honey. Then again, if you don't use *water,* what's left is the very ingredient doctors say soothes the cough in the first place: honey.

Math time: The commercial syrup costs $6.99 for four fluid ounces. A jar of wild flower honey costs $4.69 for sixteen ounces, or 400 percent more cough-soothing honey. You're paying nearly 50 percent more for 400 percent less in order to soothe your child's throat with watered-down honey, which, it's worth mentioning, can usually be purchased in pure form from the exact same supermarkets and pharmacies selling the cough syrup.

We also spend money on echinacea, which for kids is frequently packaged in an antique amber glass medicine bottle sealed at the top with a rubber dropper. Perhaps resembling the ones apothecaries and alchemists provided their ailing patients in days of yore. Modern doctors, however, have proven echinacea doesn't work.[4] A team of them from the University of Washington led by Dr. James A. Taylor looked at 337 kids treated for upper respiratory infections with echinacea and 370 kids who were treated with a placebo. There was no difference in the rate of severity, no difference in the number of days with peak symptoms, and no difference in the number of days with fever. There was, however one important distinction: Kids taking echinacea were more likely to develop a rash.

Other seemingly natural cold medications are adorned with sensitive and sweet messages—perhaps indicating they're packaged with love or without artificial colors. But very often, the medicine's active ingredients are the exact same as those used in every other over-the-counter cold medication.

Here's your cheat sheet:

- Acetaminophen is the same pain reliever and fever reducer used in Tylenol.

- Dextromethorphan HBr 5 mg is the same cough suppressant found in Robitussin.

- Phenylephrine HCl USP 2.5 mg is the same nasal decongestant found in Children's Triaminic Night Time Cold and Cough.

If your "natural" remedy contains these active ingredients, then it may be made without artificial coloring or flavors. That's great! But you have most certainly not discovered a therapy derived purely from the planet's sun-drenched fields or forests. You have in your hands a commercialized product with very Westernized drugs. You must carefully measure the dosage. And you cannot give it to children under four years old.

A lot of the cold medicines on the market are homeopathic remedies. Homeopathic medicines rely on active ingredients—plants, minerals, or animal parts such as duck livers, arsenic, table salt, poison ivy, bee venom—that are diluted thousands of times.

Does it work? Maybe. But even advocates of homeopathy will tell us that it's effective only if a practitioner prepares for a person a unique remedy based on individual symptoms. Many of those supporters maintain that when you're considering these medicines in a pharmacy or health food store, you're better off buying gum.

The FDA regulates homeopathy as a drug, but not for safety or effectiveness.[5] It's hard to imagine what other characteristics there are to consider in a drug's oversight, besides whether it's safe or effective. But the FDA also has marketing guidelines, in that homeopathic drugs mixed with nonhomeopathic active ingredients cannot be labeled "homeopathic."

That rule, unfortunately, didn't stop Terra-Medica, Inc. from putting penicillin in some of its homeopathic-labeled products.[6] (No wonder they cured people.) The line was later recalled. If your kid happens to have a potentially fatal penicillin allergy, this action might have come a little late.

Ear Infections

Today's infectious disease doctors warn us that overuse of antibiotics can result in the growth of antibiotic-resistant bacteria. If that happens, and we ever really need to fight a severe infection, the swiftest armory known to modern medicine—penicillin or amoxicillin—won't work.

That has us in search of more natural ways to cure innocent ear infections that most kids get from colds. It's a righteous goal, for sure. But there's plenty of stuff to skip.

First, there's ear candling. The theory here is one end of a lit ear candle is placed in your child's ear, and the negative pressure suctions out wax and toxins, offering relief from ear and sinus infections. Some claim it also improves brain operations. The reality here, however, is that ear candles mean *placing an open flame next to your child's ear,* which—by natural design—is located within close proximity to his extremely flammable hair, as well as his eyes, nose, and throat—critical body parts that most medical professionals will tell us do not function better after being lit on fire.

No matter. Natural websites are still instructing their readers in the art of ear candling. It's not entirely surprising that the FDA has found no valid scientific evidence to support those claims. It's also not a huge shock to learn that the FDA has received reports of burns, perforated eardrums, and blockages that later required outpatient surgery.[7] It is, however, alarming to learn that:

- Anyone even tried this in the first place;
- So many people tried it that the government—mind you, the very same government that lets us take supplements that may or may not be safe or effective—felt compelled to stand up and say *please stop trying it;*
- Ear candling continues to be touted by natural websites, health food stores, flea markets, health spas, salons, and commercial web sites for children and babies—people who *notoriously* go back on promises not to move their heads.

Adjustments to your child's vertebrae are also sold as alternatives to antibiotics in the event of chronic ear infections. Chiropractors tell us that during the birthing process, some vertebrae can become misaligned and this can affect the eustachian tube in the ears, where fluid builds up. The chiropractor manipulates the neck in ways that help drain the inner or middle ear. Most chiropractors recommend between six and eight treatments, each costing money. How much? Hard to say; it would depend on where you live.

I personally phoned a few pediatric chiropractors to get some price estimates for this book and had some trouble getting answers. But they were excellent at asking me questions about my insurance coverage. The only information I can report here is (a) every time one medical receptionist's baby gets an ear infection, her boss cures it with an adjustment, and (b) doctors' offices won't give prices for insurance-related deals, which we will discuss in great detail later.

Dr. Wurm, however—along with the Mayo Clinic's website—says we should save even the smallest copay, as there are no rigorous long-term studies to prove chiropractic adjustments work for ear infections. There is a 1997 study published in the *Journal of Clinical Chiropractic Pediatrics,* in which 332 children with chronic ear infections received a series of chiropractic adjustments. And after six months, says the report, nearly 80 percent of the children were ear infection–free. But to actually prove a point or be considered valid research, studies need at least *two* groups of subjects, a control group and an experimental group. The researchers in this case could have even divided up those 332 kids, giving half chiropractic treatment and the other half a different treatment or no treatment at all. Then we could compare recoveries between the two groups and declare one more effective. But this study merely falls in line with American Academy of Pediatrics findings that say 80 percent of ear infections clear up without any treatment at all.

Stress, Anxiety, Confidence, Depression

It cripples a parent's heart to see his or her child feeling stressed, depressed, or without confidence. Any of us would be willing to take remarkable measures to help build emotional security for our children. But when things aren't going as planned, and we as parents are worried, it would seem that a side effect–free, all-natural tonic could serve as the ideal solution. The kid would feel magically better while avoiding the stigma of antidepressants, doctors, and medical records. Sign us up.

There is no shortage of mental health supplements on the market. But sometimes they incorporate herbs that later we learn are harmful. Other times, just the potential side effects can have adverse affects. And clearly, there are times we're just plain wasting money and waiting for cures when we could be taking productive and proactive measures.

Take kava extract, which is derived from a plant native to the South Pacific, where it's been used for centuries to cure anxiety. In the United States and around the world, kava has been used for decades as an antidepressant. By one 1997 report from the *Nutrition Business Journal,* kava sales in the United States were expected to reach $50 million the following year. Today, you can spend as much as $280 for the root extract or $51 on the liquid extract, and kava products are available in countless stores. This is true despite our country's highest-level health organizations linking it to liver damage even when taken in regular doses, and even within short-term use, says the National Institutes of Health.[8] The good news is the liver damage may be reversible! It was banned from the market in Switzerland, Germany, and Canada.

Or say your kid lacks confidence. To repair this, as well as fear, stress eating, or depression, you can buy a remedy created by a company named for the late Dr. Bach. This guy practiced medicine as a surgeon in 1917, at which point he was treated for cancer and then went on to outlive his medical prognosis by twenty years. Today, the box of his confidence remedy states that it's made with larch, which according to the package instills a greater sense of self-esteem. There's little doubt that this tonic builds confidence, as FDA allows for higher levels of alcohol to be used in homeopathic medicines[9] and this one is preserved in brandy. I too find that brandy does wonders for my confidence. Scotch is even better. But there's probably a reason booze is generally illegal for kids. The company told me in an email the amount—two drops—of liquor is small enough to ignore. That's probably true.

As for larch? The active ingredient in this remedy, the company tells me, is an energy from the plant, not a physical substance. There is no evidence that plant energy can cause harm. The NIH, the FDA, and the NCCAM do not maintain reports, research, or studies on larch or its "energy." I am unqualified to discuss either one. But I think we can all agree that positive affirmations such as, *After sipping this medicine I will have more confidence* can dramatically improve a person's outlook. So buy confidence remedy if you want. But at the rate we'd burn through these little bottles costing $12.99, and the time we spend picking them up at the store, we could instead be taking our kids out for frozen yogurt. It's a great place to discuss their fears or insecurities. *And* create our own positive affirmations. *And* build an emotional foundation for their confidence. Rather than an herbal one.

For mild teen depression, many pediatricians will have their patients take Saint-John's-wort, the extract of a wild growing plant with yellow flowers used in many dietary supplements and believed to alleviate apathy or low-grade fatigue. European studies have proven it most certainly does. But in 2002 the NIH performed a four-year, $6 million study involving 340 participants and a conventional as well as alternative medicine expert named Dr. Jonathan R. T. Davidson from Duke University Medical Center. Their research concludes that Saint-John's-wort is no better than a placebo.

Either way, there is one fact doctors know for sure: Saint-John's-wort causes many drugs to work less effectively. And birth control pills are among this group of medications. It's a medical discovery to pass along to any teen taking this herb. We all want to know absolutely everything about our kids, most particularly what they're doing when we're not around. And while the idea of our kids keeping grown-up secrets from us is dreaded, the consequences of an unwanted pregnancy are even more so.

In the meantime, we have to understand that herbal remedies are celebrated on natural websites and in stores, promising to cure almost anything that ails our children. Bed-wetting, asthma, colic, bruises can all—if you believe the claims—have a simple, naturally correctable counterpart. Some can help. Others are harmless but a waste of money. And many have been found incite seizures, damage livers, and distribute toxins.

Because this is a money book, not a medical one, you won't find the potential help or harm for every herbal remedy parents are presented. The point is only to take us behind a few labels and into some labs to learn a bit about what goes untold to us in our altruistic quest to keep our kids healthy naturally. None of us *wants* to spend money off our health plans and out of pocket to ensure our kids get well with plants, not prescriptions. But it's easy to throw away a lot of money on claims that aren't tested, proven, regulated, or even perhaps safe. And that's enough to make any parent feel sick.

Tips to Avoid Wasting Money on Natural Medicine

As parents, a growing group of us prefer plants to prescriptions. The problem is that these are sold as supplements, which are not regulated for safety or effectiveness. That means you have to trust the company making, marketing, and—don't kid yourself—profiting from this $33 billion market. We'll need a whole lotta trust. Before you waste money on a product that could cost you your health, the FDA suggests we learn the following red flags:

"All natural." Some plants found in nature (such as poisonous mushrooms) can kill when consumed, so *natural* doesn't always mean *beneficial.* Moreover, the FDA has found numerous products promoted as "all natural" that contain hidden and dangerously high doses of prescription drug ingredients or even untested active artificial ingredients.

One product does it all. Be suspicious of products that claim to cure a wide range of diseases. A New York firm claimed its products marketed as dietary supplements could treat or cure senile dementia; brain atrophy; atherosclerosis; kidney dysfunction; gangrene; depression; osteoarthritis; dysuria; and lung, cervical, and prostate cancer. In October 2012, at the FDA's request, US marshals seized these products.

Personal testimonials. Success stories, such as, *It cured my diabetes* or, *My tumors are gone* are easy to make up and are not a substitute for scientific evidence.

Quick fixes. Few diseases or conditions can be treated quickly, even with legitimate products. Beware of language such as, *Lose 30 pounds in 30 days,* or *Eliminates skin cancer in days.*

"Miracle cure." Alarms should go off when you see this claim or others like it such as *new discovery, scientific breakthrough, or secret ingredient.* If a real cure for a serious disease were discovered, it would be widely reported through the media and prescribed by health professionals—not buried in print ads, TV infomercials, or Internet sites.

Conspiracy theories. Claims like, *The pharmaceutical industry and the government are working together to hide information about a miracle cure* are always untrue and unfounded. These statements are used to distract consumers from the obvious, common-sense questions about the so-called miracle cure.

(Source: US Food and Drug Administration http://www.fda.gov/drugs/emergencyprepared-ness/bioterrorismanddrugpreparedness/ucm137284.htm)

Raise Them Better for Less

Those of us seeking holistic cures aren't necessarily in need of expensive alternatives to conventional doctors and medicine. Just like the earth's most natural resources, the most effective remedies are cheap and readily available.

IMMUNE SYSTEM

The first and most beneficial way to protect our kids from prescriptions, doctors, and dangerous herbs is to prevent them from getting sick in the first place. And the key is to build super-strong immune systems that can fight infection and disease, says Dr. Gwen Wurm. We would do well to spend even their healthy days constructing strong bodies with vegetables, fruits, and proteins.

For babies, of course, this means breast-feeding. I, for one, did not get off to a great start in this department. But I'm here to report the facts, not to praise corporate America for providing the welcome solution of infant formula to the good mothers who for various and very understandable reasons did not breast-feed. (The FDA conducts yearly inspections of all formula manufacturing facilities and collects and analyzes product samples.) For toddlers, children, and teens, you start Operation Strong Body simply by deciding on a few disease-fighting foods each day. Want to ward off depression? The omega-3 fatty acids in fish have been found to lower levels of apathy. The vital nutrients in broccoli and kale work at detoxifying the liver. The fats in avocados coat our neurons, meaning the brain fires signals off faster. We can thwart colds and flu with soups flavored by garlic, onions, and leeks, which are known to boost human immune systems. Our digestive tracks work better when powered with the good bacteria in yogurt. And our blood flow is improved by the magnesium in almonds. You get the idea.

SLEEP

Though perhaps we might never in our whole lives have imagined being *this* tired, our kids need sleep even more than we do. Shut-eye isn't just the fantastic gift of time our kids give us to catch up on emails. It's also nature's magical—and since the subject here is money, I'll point out *free*—way of preventing and healing a host of physical issues that store-bought remedies only claim to cure. Researchers have piles of evidence on sleep, as it appears they have no problem depriving people of it and watching to see what happens.

Sometimes, the subjects develop a tendency to get fat. Scientists at the University of Chicago in 1999 limited eleven healthy young adults to four hours' sleep for six nights and found they were less able to process sugar, in some cases to the level of diabetics.[10] A lack of sleep interrupts hormone production, increasing ghrelin levels (which makes us feel hungry) and decreasing the levels of leptin (which makes us feel satisfied), says Dr. Wurm. What's more, when the human body is tired, it mistakes its need for sleep as a craving for sugary foods. Being tired also doesn't do much for a kid's enthusiasm about joining the volleyball team.

Sleep and mood are closely related, meaning healthy slumber can prevent mild depression and boost a kid's happiness and, potentially, her self-confidence. The National Sleep Foundation in 2006 polled children ages eleven to seventeen years old and found that 73 percent of adolescents who reported being unhappy also did not get enough sleep.[11] At the University of Pennsylvania, researchers limited subjects to just 4.5 hours of sleep.[12] Afterward, these people reported feeling stressed, angry, sad, and mentally exhausted—most of which disappeared when they returned to normal schedules. (In the event anyone cares, I could personally report those exact same results after every holiday season.) A decline in serotonin levels is among the hormonal commotion occurring when a person lacks sleep. And that hormone plays a big role in controlling depression, says Dr. Wurm.

Sleep Strategy

Here are the guidelines for how many hours per day your child should be sleeping according to advice from Dr. Gwen Wurm:

Age	Hours of Sleep
Babies (0–3 months)	14–17
Infants (4–11 months)	12–15
Toddlers (1–2 years)	11–14
3–5 years old	10–13
6–13 years old	9–11
14–17 years old	8–10

We may have to put in some serious parenting here, because the children who benefit most from sleep's many advantages are those who have bedtime-related rules, according to the National Sleep Foundation. Most notably: an actual bedtime. After that, some parents have taken drastic—even unthinkable (if you're a teenager)—measures, such as making kids shut off their phones and televisions at the same time *every night*. Other parents even have a cut-off time for caffeinated drinks. Tough love.

DOING NOTHING

When it comes to ear infections, doctors say there is one natural cure with an 80 percent success rate: doing absolutely nothing. Yes, it turns out we are all qualified to be experts on curing ear infections, since the American Academy of Pediatrics in 2013 made "doing nothing" the official course of action for an otherwise healthy kid who has an ear infection.[13] This move came after studies proved that 80 percent of them go away by themselves.

Even better, we can naturally prevent ear infections from developing in the first place, says Dr. Wurm. For kids who are allergic, ridding our homes of allergens—dust, mold, cats (her advice, not mine)—can reduce the risk of developing ear infections. While we're at it, we can't let the kid drink bottles lying down or smoke around her.

Even with healthy diets and fluid-free ears, our kids are going to catch colds—and the most effective natural medicines are the most simple. "We have to accept the fact that viral illnesses are a normal part of being on this planet," says Dr. Wurm. "We'll care for kids and keep them hydrated but we don't have to spend tons of money on medicines for cold symptoms." Honey is great for soothing coughs in kids over twelve months, says the AAP. We can give it by the spoonful almost as often as necessary, and buckwheat honey is a choice variety. To clear up congestion, we can squirt saline drops in their noses. And the best remedy for stuffy sinuses is steam, says Dr. Wurm. That means turning on the shower, shutting the bathroom door, and holding your baby while the room fills up with healing vapor. This will help the kid breathe better, which will help him sleep better, which will fight the cold.

COMPLETE WELLNESS

It seems nature is highly therapeutic when you can see it, as dozens of studies prove that simply being in and around green space can have dramatic benefits on a person's mental and physical well-being. Outdoor play increases a child's level of vitamin D, which protects against future bone problems, heart disease, and diabetes. It also gives kids better distance vision, says Dr. Wurm. Natural surroundings can also protect kids from stress, according to Cornell University researchers, who in 2003 found that kids who lived and played among the most plants inside and around their homes responded with less psychological distress to traumatic events.[14] What's more, the kids with the most stress also got the most out of being in nature. And there is no ceiling effect—meaning the more nature the kid saw, the better that kid could handle stress.

Dr. Wurm's patients never disagree with the findings, but they do argue about whether there's time each day for outdoor play. Dr. Wurm suggested to one father who picks his kids up from school that he arrive at dismissal with sandwiches. On the way to the next destination—basketball, tutoring, or home—he can stop at a park where the kids eat and play for a half hour. This works for a kid being picked up from anywhere. Parents of kids who ride buses will have to create a custom green-space strategy. But this is proven to be an effective investment in time, not in money. And all natural, all around.

When my babies were actual babies, we together took a baby massage class. Proponents of baby massage say that it promotes restful sleep, boosts the immune system, helps digestion, balances respiration, and stimulates the production of oxytocin, a hormone that works as a pain reliever. I have no idea whether this is true or whether there are studies to back it up. I do know that most people—including baby people—find massages to be relaxing. As parents, this gives us the opportunity to focus on our kids' tiny toes and their chubby little nine-month-old legs. Perhaps the most important thing I learned in our baby massage class is that you don't need a baby massage class to gently apply cream to your baby's feet and arms. This exercise is free to learn and free to practice.

When babies become children, meditation is another risk-free, low-cost, and very natural way to lower blood pressure, reduce stress, decrease anxiety, and instill an improved sense of well-being, says Dr. Wurm. The evidence of these health benefits is still in its early stages. But the investments in such returns are so small it hardly matters. Meditating is an indisputably calming bedtime ritual that requires approximately five minutes and zero dollars. There is no shortage of free online resources. You'll certainly want to choose your downloads carefully, but that's only because it would be embarrassing to get a computer virus from someone pretending to care about inner peace. Not because any particular meditating technique is harmful.

Rock-Solid Money Move

It's true: Just because a few herb-makers have messed up doesn't mean we should avoid prescribing and testing. It certainly doesn't mean we should give up learning to navigate the health insurance system, not an easy feat. We must study up on the playbook so we don't get beaten down by a system so much bigger than any one person. By learning to avoid some of the insurance companies' sneakiest snags, along with a few guidelines from doctors and lawmakers, we can recover from being sick and still maintain good financial health. By learning to partner with our physicians in our quest for our kids' good health, we can most effectively heal our kids.

Your Rock-Solid Money Move is to become an expert on the finances of health care, which I realize might not be exactly what you felt like doing today. But it gets exciting later on. Because mastering this game lets you walk away with money.

There's a lot of ground to cover. Just as a holistic approach considers the whole person, your health insurance covers the whole family. That's why we have to understand the potential pitfalls within both pediatric and adult care. They could cost you tens or even hundreds of thousands of dollars.

Overtesting

Some people say they lost trust—and money—in the practice of modern medicine because unnecessary tests and treatments are too quickly inscribed on our charts and then later on our credit cards. (Before complaining about this, be sure you're not the parent who—even accidentally—pushed your doctor in this direction.) This practice isn't just wasting resources; it's exposing the whole family to more poking and prodding. It turns out much of the medical community completely agrees. *Consumer Reports,* which has for years tested for us the quality of products, has begun to focus on health care. It's looking at the performance, cost, and safety of these services in a campaign in collaboration with the ABIM Foundation it calls "Choosing Wisely." The watchdog group is talking to patients, digging through insurance complaints, and teaming up with medical groups representing family practice doctors, internists, cardiologists, radiologists, and many others. In its article, "When to Say 'Whoa' to Your Doctor," *Consumer Reports* points to the Congressional Budget Office, which said up to 30 percent of the health care in the United States is unnecessary. It holds up a Dartmouth College survey stating that about half of primary care physicians say their own patients get too much medical care.[1]

Too much medical care, it turns out, can be very bad for your health. For example, when EKGs, which record the heart's electrical activity, are done on people without chest pain or those who are high-risk patients, they often lead to follow-up CT angiograms, which expose patients to a radiation dose equal to six hundred to eight hundred chest X-rays, says *Consumer Reports*.

Sometimes, the pain is better than the medical investigation. Imaging tests for lower back pain, for example, can cost up to $1,500 and will zap a person's reproductive system with radiation. For those who get headaches and want a CT scan, you should know these tests can reveal things that appear worrisome but aren't, says *Consumer Reports*. Follow-up tests can be endless and expensive. And DEXA scans routinely used to diagnose weak bones in women have the potential to reveal only mild bone loss (called osteopenia) which carries a very low risk for bone fracture. Treating it, however, involves medication with a long list of side effects: difficulty swallowing, bone loss in the jaw, abnormal heart rhythm.

Kids' eyes are also overtested. It turns out they don't need comprehensive eye exams each year, says *Consumer Reports* in *Choosing*

---

1. The information from Consumers Union in this chapter is protected by copyright as follows: © Consumers Union of U.S., Inc. Yonkers, NY 10703-1057, the nonprofit publisher of Consumer Reports. Excerpted with permission from *Choosing Wisely, When to Say 'Whoa' to Doctors*, May 2012, *Vision Care for Children* May 2014; *That CT scan costs how much?* July 2012; *Surprise medical bills are costing consumers* May 2015; *Viewpoint: Improving the marketplace for consumers*, April 2015 for educational purposes only. No commercial use or reproduction permitted. www.ConsumerReports.org

Wisely article, "Vision Care for Children." Those cost between $100 and $200, and a $20 routine eye exam is enough. Most don't need retinal imaging tests and they certainly don't need a "baseline" test to compare with future tests. (*Consumer Reports* puts quotes around the word *baseline,* making me think they'd heard *that* one a few times.)

The thing about doctor's orders is we're supposed to follow them, not question them—even though it's perfectly reasonable to do so. Your doctor, of course, will give better medical advice than what's printed in a money book. The caution here is to open our eyes before we open our wallets.

COST COMPARISONS

You know to have tests or exams done by providers in your network, but here's something the medical community doesn't typically broadcast: The various doctors and hospitals in your network charge very different rates for the same exact services—even when being paid by the same exact insurance company—says *Consumer Reports*. This can cost or save you a lot of money if you have coinsurance or if you have not met your deductible. Say, for example, you're slated to have an uncomplicated vaginal delivery. If you had an Aetna PPO and lived in Hartford, Connecticut, this would cost $5,249 at one hospital and $8,941 at another very close by, *Consumer Reports* uncovered in its 2012 article "That CT Scan Costs How Much?" If you had a typical coinsurance responsibility of 20 percent, this would be an out-of-pocket difference amounting to $738. This is true for all medical services, from check-ups to lab results to surgery. Price ranges are particularly broad for services such as MRIs and CT scans, says *Consumer Reports*. They typically cost thousands of dollars more at hospitals than they do at imaging centers.

You may be able to learn the rates for all service providers online. Then again, you may not. In such cases you would revert to an ancient practice dating back to a time before Sergey Brin invented Google: calling your insurance provider on the phone. That way, you can ask about prices charged by individual physicians and labs. Don't bother phoning your doctor for this information, says *Consumer Reports*. Most physicians are not particularly eager to give away their rates. Some even prohibit the insurance companies from disclosing them. Perhaps that's because most offices negotiate countless fee plans among many insurance companies. This is exactly why I could not get the chiropractors to give me an exact price.

Even when we think we're armed with information, we could accidentally use medical care outside of our networks without even knowing. We discover this only with the arrival of a colossal medical bill. *Consumer Reports* calls these "surprise medical bills," and rest assured, these could happen to any of us.

The most obvious scenario involves having a heart attack or other medical emergency near a hospital that doesn't accept our policies. This situation is tempered slightly by the Affordable Care Act, which made it illegal for our health plans to charge us higher copays or coinsurance than it does for in-network emergency services. The plan can't require us to get preauthorization and it can't demand extra administrative hurdles.

But it doesn't stop doctors from billing us. And don't worry, they will. Something called balance billing means a doctor charges the insurance company her fee, accepts the portion paid by the insurer, and then bills us, the patient, for the rest, says *Consumer Reports* in its 2015 article, "Surprise Medical Bills Are Costing Consumers." We can't blame a professional for collecting her rates. But it's easy to become infuriated to learn this happens at hospitals that *do* accept our policies.

See, the tricky thing about the inner workings of insurance coverage within hospitals is, well, everything. Hospitals are not monolithic organizations with standardized insurance contracts and billing arrangements that are easily transferable across all departments and practices. Rather, when it comes to payments and insurance contracts, hospitals are a system of cross-wired chaos in which some of the wires aren't even connected to anything at all. Very few people who physically work in hospitals are even employees of the hospital. Most of them are private practices with private insurance company contracts.

So after being admitted to your insurance-friendly emergency department and being examined by an insurance-friendly physician, it may be decided that you now—and by "now" they mean *now*—require the care of a cardiologist or a plastic surgeon. You, let's remember, will likely be preoccupied with the life-threatening emergency at hand. It may slip your mind to, say, request a specialist who accepts your insurance plan. You might also, given the chest pains or missing finger, be feeling at that moment a bit vulnerable. Heck, you may even be unconscious. And that's how it happens: The specialist or team of specialists arrive immediately to provide you with urgent medical care. These people apply their decades of medical training to sewing your head back on. And then they want to get paid. You can't blame them. But you're left with sometimes tens of thousands of dollars' worth of bills. Even though you're insured. And even though you went to a medical facility accepting your insurance.

Perhaps we're in need of administrative fixes or legislative ones, and lawmakers say they're trying. Some thirteen states have very strict laws about balance billing and surprise bills. In New York, for example, medical providers must notify patients before treatment if they don't take their insurance.[15] If not, patients will be required to pay a regular copay, as if the provider was in network.

The ACA also cracked down on insurance companies, in hopes of getting fair payments for those who provide emergency care. The thinking is that if doctors are paid adequately by the insurance companies—the people who are supposed to pay them—then their patients will be less likely to receive big bills.[16] The reality, however, is that doctors and lawmakers won't likely agree on the dollar amount of "adequate." But at least insurance companies have to pay out-of-network emergency providers the greatest of three amounts: (1) the amount it pays in-network providers, (2) a payment based on the same methods the plan uses to pay for other out-of-network services, or (3) the amount Medicare would pay for that service.

There seems to have been much less progress made on the risk of inadvertently hiring out-of-network doctors in surgical situations. Concert pianist Claudia Knafo told *Consumer Reports* she thought she chose an in-network surgeon. Her doctor's office photographed her insurance card and said everything was fine. Perhaps it was for them. But Knafo got a bill for $101,000 and later spent seven months disputing it. In my own research, I found that these complaints are pretty common. It's even more common for patients to say that they woke up and recovered only to learn the anesthesiologist did not work with their insurance.

In some instances you'll intentionally use doctors who don't accept your insurance plan, perhaps because you found one specializing in a rare condition, or a professional you simply trust. Check your insurance documents, because many plans will agree to pay a percent of a rate that they've decided is fair and reasonable. Again, there is a chance your doctor and your insurance company will not agree on this amount.

That means it's a good idea to figure out the cost in advance. If your insurance company thinks $1,000 is a fair and reasonable rate for the procedure, agreeing to pay 60 percent of that, but your doctor thinks that $2,000 is a fair and reasonable rate for the procedure, the insurance company won't care. You'll get $600. Some doctors may be willing to work with us on the costs of treatments. We can get ideas about high, low, and average rates for almost every medical service at FAIR Health Consumer (fairhealthconsumer.org) or Healthcare Blue Book (healthcarebluebook.com) and reference those amounts when considering our choices.

If your insurance company denies a claim, the ACA also made it legal to appeal this decision. We can request the company reconsider when it (1) says the care is not medically necessary or appropriate, (2) says you are not eligible for the health plan or benefit, (3) you have a preexisting condition, or (4) the care is experimental or investigational. Instructions on how to file an appeal should arrive with the denial of payment. You've got to prepare a good case. Get the plan's file on your claim—including the evidence and guidelines it used in making the original decision. And dispute those conclusions with letters from your doctor and findings from medical journals. You can even ask a customer assistance program to help you. If it's still denied, your next step is to appeal to an independent reviewer, such as a state insurance department or a private, independent review organization that has no reason to favor your insurance company. You can expect a decision in forty-five days. It's final, unless your insurance company takes the matter to court. In that case, you'll have legal fees on top of your medical liabilities.

Online Resources That Could Save Your Financial Life

Consumer Reports, "How to Avoid Unnecessary Tests and Treatments" (www.consumerreports.org/cro/2012/04/choosing-wisely-how-to-avoid-unnecessary-tests-and-treatments).

This article teaches us how to avoid unnecessary medical treatments and costs.

Consumer Reports has excellent information on health insurance, whether you are covered by your employer, are on Medicare, or buy insurance on your own. To find that information, go to www.ConsumerReports.org/healthinsurance.

HealthCare.gov (www.healthcare.gov)

The URL says it all—this is the government's site on health care. If you have employment-based coverage and don't like it, look here to find your options: www.healthcare.gov/have-job-based-coverage.

National Association of Insurance Commissioners
(www.naic.org/state_web_map.htm)

Here's where to compare companies and complain.

Consumer Health Choices (http://consumerhealthchoices.org)

This site offers free resources for sensible health care decisions:

- See ratings by state and what people are saying about your doctor before it's too late (http://consumerhealthchoices. org/patients-and-consumers/#doctors).

- See prices for medical services (http://consumerhealth- choices.org/patients-and-consumers/#price-reports)

- Lower your costs when it comes to taking medicine (http:// consumerhealthchoices.org/patients-and-consumers/ #drugs-and-supplements).

CHAPTER EIGHT

Materialism

choose
STYLISH FREEDOM
OVER BRAND-NAME SLAVERY

Save Unlimited Amounts of Money

The Stuff You'll Skip

It's endless and unlimited.

Let's say it's worth $1 million over eighteen years.

Or $2 million.

Maybe more.

I f you're anything like my friend Laurie, your kids live in the land of $100 sneakers, and yeah, most of their classmates own more than one pair. (Most people call this land "America.") And in these neighborhoods that are magically affluent—because prosperity can be an illusion—designer labels make daily appearances on babies, children, tweens, and teens. Not to mention their luxury car–driving parents.

So if you're Laurie, and overcompensating for your recent divorce, you will smile and put the occasional pair of Nike sneakers on your credit card. And as your son becomes a teen you may notice a change: He starts to care about his appearance—even above his feet. At first you'll find this wonderful—Laurie did—because her son Sean started showering. (Voluntarily.) Sean also got a job and used his paychecks to buy preppy designer shirts from Lacoste and Brooks Brothers. Also wonderful, thought Laurie. But late one afternoon, Laurie, who had long ago assigned Sean the job of doing his own laundry, went into her son's closet and made a shocking discovery. The kid owned seventeen pairs of Sperry Top-Siders. He had acquired more than sixty dress and polo shirts, many of which he was storing on the closet floor in crumpled shirt balls. And he had countless preppy whale belts, some still strangling khaki pant loops and others that lay lifeless, flat on the floor.

It was like a rack of black leather jackets had broken into the closet to commit a preppy apparel massacre. But in reality the closet represented what was becoming the slow demise of Sean's emotional state.

The designer clothes at first launched him into the same league as the richer kids at school. But with his job and control over a paycheck, he soon surpassed them—fashionably speaking, anyway. Fueled with confidence, Sean started taking style risks that set school-wide trends.

He was the first kid to wear an argyle sweater, and after his friends followed, Sean began a seemingly eternal hunt for hard-to-find golf shirts, zooming in on his grandfather's membership to an exclusive country club selling its namesake apparel.

While teens throughout time have relied on clothing to tell the world their social standing—the greasers, the cheerleaders—Sean was no longer testing out a persona; instead he had slid into every textbook definition of being materialistic. He believed that the acquisition of designer labels would bring personal improvement. He was acquiring possessions as a means of establishing his self-worth. And he held the mistaken belief that the most exclusive and expensive items were the route toward happiness.

The problem with raising materialistic children is that they grow up to be materialistic adults. Psychologists and marketing researchers have long established materialistic people are more anxious, more depressed, and more likely to use drugs and alcohol.[1] They're more likely to be in debt and less likely to have happy marriages. People who agree with the statement, *some of the most important achievements in life include acquiring material possessions* are the least satisfied with life. Don't worry; no one here is going to preach the practice of relinquishing all our worldly possessions. As for my kids, I'd like *them* to grow up and earn money (I certainly don't want them asking me for any). Because while researchers prove that lottery winners return to their regular levels of baseline happiness after a year, they also say that those who can't afford food aren't jumping with joy, either.

If Sean seemed pretty happy in the moment, you have to know that whale belts are not a sustainable form of fulfillment. (And not just because most Americans find them ugly.) Materialism and its corresponding (not to mention constant) quest for acquisitions puts people on what psychologists Philip Brickman and Donald Campbell termed "the hedonic treadmill." We will most certainly get pleasure from every purchase; that's the hedonistic part. But it doesn't last long, so we need to buy more stuff—or make more money—to maintain the same level of happiness.

The kids with the best wardrobes and the fanciest toys are simply not the ones squeezing the most joy out of each day. At least not because of all the stuff they own. That gets boring very quickly. Psychologists have agreed that the human brain is built to adapt to its surroundings. It's the reason people who live near railroad tracks don't notice the walls rattling from the roar of the trains. It's why people can cope with great tragedy and go on to later experience joy. And it's why our kids so quickly grow bored of their new sneakers or new toy. No matter the length of time the kid longed for the sneakers, regardless of the time she'd spent shopping for them, or how many commercials she watched promoting them, sneakers are stagnant items: They don't change or grow or become more interesting.[2] It's a quick countdown after buying them until the kid becomes accustomed to owning them. And in a matter of days—maybe even a week—it feels like they'd been sitting in her closet forever. Boring.

No matter how much money you have, keeping a retail buzz going is exhausting, emotionally and financially. We either work so much we skip out on more fulfilling activities, such as learning languages and being with friends, or we go into debt, racking up huge credit card bills. Both are excellent ways to make yourself miserable. Anyone—rich or poor—with a laser-sharp focus on labels is likely to make choices that will chip away at what would be an otherwise satisfying life.

Perhaps the worst part about our kids being materialistic is that it's largely our fault. We can try to blame others, and there are no shortage of scapegoats. The school, for example, should have a uniform. Social media, of course, provides a platform for bragging. Compounding the problem is the fact that material goods are designed for comparison. There's a numerical dollar value—a system that's created for the sole purpose of evaluation—assigned to each logo. And our brains are trained to evaluate those relationships.

But science proves that for the most part it's a kid's parents who are responsible for even accidentally teaching the kid that whoever has the most stuff wins. Often, we don't even know we're doing this. But while our kids might be a bit influenced by their friends, it's actually us, their parents, that help shape their attitudes about whether store-bought stuff will make them happy or cause people to like them more.

So what are we doing? Well, very few of us sit down to breakfast each day and remind our children to please make friends with the kids wearing the most expensive clothes. Perhaps some of us, however, may realize that we're giving our kids materialistic gifts in place of emotional support, only temporarily because we've been busy working or getting divorced or whatever else might be preventing us from quality parenting. And most of us are well aware that our kids model our behavior. We know we're transmitting values, whether we happen to be constantly acquiring new purses or electing political candidates or volunteering at nonprofit organizations.

Even though, say, buying your kid a video game because you're too busy to take him to the park for a few days doesn't sound like the worst idea in the world, most extreme and intentional material-ist parenting probably doesn't relate to any of us. We're good people, right? We have good values. We care about books and exercise and emotions. We go on *hikes*, for God's sake. But even during our most deliberate intentions to emphasize to our kids quality endeavors such as school and sports and philanthropy, we could unknowingly be planting materialistic seeds. Rewarding our kids for good behavior with material goods—telling both ourselves and our children that they'd earned their gifts—can have some undesired affects, according to research from Lan Nguyen Chaplin from the University of Illinois, who studied materialism and parenting and learned that rewards have powerful effects on shaping our kids' behavior.[3] While rewards may motivate our kids to behave in ways we find desirable, they do come with the tiny problem of perhaps reducing the emphasis on the skill and increasing the focus on the new cell phone or the downloaded app or whatever it is we gave them. The reward may send a message saying that the satisfaction you get from accomplishing the goal is not sufficient. Earning As in school is great! And your new cell phone completes the effort.

To find out how rewards and other material aspects of parenting affect our kids, Chaplin and her fellow researchers studied more than five hundred young people. They dug deep into those childhoods, assessing parental support in the form of emotions, rewards, punishments, and privileges. They assessed happiness levels throughout the years, as well as insecurities and emphasis on buying things that other people notice or admire.

And they found that the people who had received many material rewards as kids were pretty darn likely as adults to associate any accomplishments with the acquisition of store-bought goods. This may not seem a great psychological tragedy. As parents, we all might like to see our kids earn sufficient financial rewards in exchange for hard work. But if our kids judge another person's success and competency based on the handbag she carries, it's our child who will likely miss out on valuable friendships. If our kids become accustomed to getting rewards for each accomplishment, they could rack up debt before they even *get* rich. What's more, experts have long established that being driven by extrinsic forces—those coming from the outside world, as opposed to internal motivation—will make a person less inspired to put forth any effort when there are no rewards, such as when it comes to charity or other prosocial projects. Those are proven to bring people permanent happiness.

The researchers also figured there were two ways to be materialistic. Warm and loving parents can bestow upon their kids a well-deserved reward. But those children tended to believe that when you do something great, you get a commercialized compensation. But if kids grew up believing they'd disappointed their parents, they would suffer from a more evil form of materialism: the belief they'd be happier if only they owned more—and better—stuff. Even those of us with limited psychology training can diagnose the random Ferrari driver of trying to fill an emotional void.

But wait, there's more. We don't bestow great gifts on our kids only when they do something great; we also give them "unconditional gifts," just because their faces are so darn cute when they get something they've wanted for even an hour of their tiny, little lives. They delight in receiving these things. We delight in their delight. It's too bad there's scientific proof that all this delight can be harmful. Here's how: In addition to developing behaviors, kids are also in the midst of acquiring identities, the researchers say. They discover a lot about themselves when navigating social relationships and making friends, but they also learn who they are by the way other people respond to them. If teachers say they're smart or their friends compliment their athleticism, those remarks will help shape their own sense of self. But guess what? The clothes a child wears or the electronic gadgets he holds can also help create his identity, the researchers say.

The kids who were showered with conditional and unconditional rewards were more likely to grow up expecting that these things could improve their own self-concepts. They believed they'd be more attractive to others if they accumulated more material goods. As adults, these people placed emphasis on possessions as a means to develop and transform their identities.

At this point, you at this point may be feeling one—or all—of the following:

1. Schadenfreude in the knowledge that the huge collection of designer clothes the neighborhood kid owns will one day make her as miserable as they've been making you for the past six years.
2. Relief to have discovered scientific support for the idea of not buying your kids things.
3. Confusion, because now we can't, like, buy them anything *ever?*

We can.

Listen, our kids don't just want nice things, they also need them. We can't be functional members of an organized society and take our kids to first communions or bat mitzvahs in their school uniforms. (Talk about your psychological scars.) So I contacted Chaplin, admitted I'd been messing up my daughters, and asked her professional opinion on when we could safely spend money.

Turns out, we can give them things every now and again so long as we deliver these gifts with a side of healthy parenting. With each reward or Because-They're-Cute present (my term, not the scientific one) we have to remind them to be grateful, says Chaplin. Gratitude helps combat materialism, she says, while also promoting happiness. We also have to teach them to give to others, so they're not always on the receiving end. What's more, we can give our kids gifts, but we can't use them as substitutes for paying attention to them, which not incidentally means I need an entirely new parenting plan during my book tour. Hanging up our cell phones, ignoring our emails, and returning texts much later—scratch that, I'll need a new parenting plan for this afternoon—will also provide the warmth and support they need to thrive.

It's not bad to have a lot of money or to spend a lot of money (it sounds awesome, actually), but it brings little joy if it's a person's primary achievement. Psychologists and researchers tell us that materialistic kids—adults too, of course—invest in goods to compensate for doubts about their self-worth.[4] Materialism is a coping strategy, they say, that people use to satisfy unmet emotional needs. Low self-esteem has been long linked to materialism in people of all ages. Think about it. If you don't feel particularly valuable as a person, a pair of Nike sneakers is a great way to inform the world of your significance. A kid who's overly concerned with the number of dresses she has in comparison to her best friend is manifesting insecurity. Not style. Not love. Not support.

That's another thing: Chaplin's study of over one hundred adolescents between the ages of twelve and eighteen years old showed that when a parent concentrates on status items—perhaps even treating her kids as one—the child's self-esteem will suffer.[5] That's right. Parents and peers can impact kids' level of materialism with an influence even more powerful then presents—our influence on their self-esteem. And while materialistic parents and friends have been known to produce materialistic kids, this research studied whether the effect penetrated deeper than the transmission of values, peer pressure, and competition to actually influence self-esteem.

It does.

The researchers found through their study that kids with supportive parents, even materialistic ones, were less likely to believe that happiness could be purchased at the mall. Their sense of self was healthy; they didn't need status items to fill any voids or compensate for feelings of low self-worth. They took pride in their achievements. They were fulfilled emotionally from close relationships with family and friends. The parenting style responsible for this psychological outcome was one that encourages kids to communicate feelings. These parents respected autonomy, self-expression, and independent thinking. And while the researchers say these attributes are actually associated with all aspects of a person's social competence, including moral behavior and creativity, it's true now too, they say, that self-esteem can prevent materialism.

As for friends, most of us likely blame our kids' snotty social circles—we're not naming names here—when our own offspring are clamoring for brand names. They want to be cool, they want to both fit in and be admired. Even among scientists, social influence has always dominated the discussions about adolescents and materialism. But friends aren't just people who have good taste in clothes; they're also people who provide support for our kids. There is actually very little evidence that materialism among a kid's peers will increase adolescent materialism. Sure, children are learning the social significance of products. As I write these pages, I know that if my own daughter saw the words *Brandy Melville* stamped on a sandwich bag, she would suddenly find value in yesterday's tuna-on-rye. But there's also little evidence that kids are busy copying each other's buying patterns.

What Chaplin and her team did find is that kids who felt supported and liked by their friends were much less materialistic. They had more self-esteem, and it wasn't dependent on logos. The materialistic kids, however, had lower self-esteem and more materialistic friends, from whom they got less support, say the researchers. This could be because they're unable to compete with wealthier peers, what with their expensive and popular brand names. But it could also be, say the researchers, because materialistic kids tend to place more emphasis on possessions. And less on building strong relationships. At any rate, kids with highly materialistic friends have lower feelings of self-worth and are less likely to form strong emotional bonds.

If psychologists know anything about human happiness, it's that high-quality social relationships are our principal sources of joy. Admiring someone's argyle sweater (even if that *were* possible) or receiving such admiration does not set the foundation for the kind of altruistic and trusting friendships that fulfill a kid's emotional needs. And, kids who view clothes, cars, and money with great importance will pursue people based on their status, not their spirit. Materialistic people are also typically competitive. It's difficult being good to your friends when you're at the same time trying to beat them.

Raise Them Better for Less

So what to do? Well, no one here is going to suggest removing all Christmas toys from under the tree. American kids have the right to a somewhat commercialized childhood! We, as their parents, just have to know that constantly chasing the products companies are pushing—even if we can afford to buy every single one—will not build our children's self esteem.

You may want to punch the guy who said, "People who think money can't buy happiness don't know where to shop." But he was right, and you can actually spend your money in ways that positively impact your internal optimism. Finding happiness is a goal we all share. And so researchers have studied how we can spend money in ways that really can bring us lasting joy. And the answer has nothing to do with retail stores.

Are You Overspending in Stores?

Maybe it's not all your fault. I pulled from my newspaper column, "The Home Economist," the following five psychological traps that can trick our brains into thinking it's okay to spend money.

1. Interruptions. Say we're in the store, evaluating two video cameras, and trying to decide which to buy. Suddenly we spot a neighbor, who stops for some small talk. When turning our attention back to the cameras, we're likely to instantly pick the more expensive one, according to research from professor Wendy Liu at University of California, San Diego. That's because our brains operate under the illusion they've processed this decision previously. That makes them less attentive and, in that state of mind, ready to choose the item with better features. All interruptions will have this effect, so don't go shopping hungry, carry some water, wear comfortable shoes, and shut off your cell phone.

2. Zeros. Our brains can barely process zeros, according to research from Mauricio Palmeira at Australia's Monash University. When we're considering interest rates or down payments (or even the fat content of food) and one of our choices is zero (as in, *none* of the undesirable) we'll likely pick the more expensive option (such as 5 percent down or 2 percent interest). It's because our brains are more comfortable comparing two actual numbers. When faced with a goose egg, it's a good idea to concentrate harder and think it all through.

3. Tediousness. Instead of thinking about the boring task of bill-paying, keep in your mind when shopping the exciting things you can do with saved money. Objectives are more likely to be met when we remember what's motivating our behavior, according to research from Sean McCrea, a psychology professor at University of Wyoming. Keep with you a list—or better yet, pictures—of your financial goals: a new house, fishing in your retirement years, or even college brochures for your kids.

4. 99s. Human beings are hardwired, when looking at prices, to consider the number furthest left, according to research from Vicki Morwitz, a marketing professor at New York University's Stern School of Business. It's the way the human brain reads, processes, and codes numbers. So for example, we'll see a $14.99 price tag and process it as $14 instead of $15. Just knowing about the bias can help you more realistically consider things before you buy them.

5. Words. Yes, even a seemingly innocent *good-bye* can trick us—if we're distracted—into thinking a product is a "good buy," according to research from Derick Davis, an assistant marketing professor at the University of Miami. They're called homophones—two words with the same pronunciation but different meanings—and they give us higher purchasing intentions and make us more willing to spend money. What can we do? The effects are strongest when we're not paying attention, so being aware this works can counteract the spell.

6. Nostalgia. Scientists have for years known that our longing for the past will have us spending money in the immediate moment, and now research from Kathleen D. Vohs at the University of Minnesota reveals why: Currency is something that connects us to our present needs, which, when we're feeling nostalgic, are not of great concern. We're particularly vulnerable during the holidays, when our childhood songs are played in stores and the smells of gingerbread are wafting everywhere. The best defense: Snap out of it. By staying in the present we can shop with one eye on our financial future.

You know what improves our lives? Yes, that's exactly right: Snickers Ice Cream Bars. Experiences, which include ice cream–eating and also travel and social occasions, will continue over time to bring us more and more satisfaction, long after they occur, says Leaf Van Boven, a professor at University of Colorado Boulder, who studied the postpsychological purchasing effects.[6] That's why we should be supplementing those store-bought gift stockpiles with those offering the real route to happiness: presents that get our kids *doing* things, not owning them.

One mom, Myra, who's a designer in Miami, got her daughter a movie app and video camera for Christmas, because she's interested in filmmaking. Another mom, Alissa, bought her kid the job of being fire chief for the day at a community fund-raiser. But all experiences from sharing a pretzel in the park to family skating rink outings will bring more lasting value than a Saturday spent shopping. It's fun at the time, of course, with the little expected headaches. But after the day's over and your kids are discussing it with friends over the phone and on the social media platform they happen to be using at the time, what's reinforced in their minds will be the hilarity of slipping around and colliding on the ice, because let's face it: Kids sliding around on ice with blades on their feet is pure comedy. For *everyone*.

Starting from a wobble, meanwhile, but then graduating to strong strides around the rink is the kind of activity that furthers what are called "intrinsic goals"—activities that offer self-satisfaction. Working on those builds a person's self-esteem and makes them happier. It's why we'll get great joy from pursuing interests that we find challenging and fun. And, experiences allow our kids to participate in what many of them already consider the only activity worth doing anyway: hanging out with their friends. If your kids can host three friends at a trampoline park, something funny is guaranteed to happen. (Perhaps even something to do with *you* attempting to jump on a trampoline.) The kids will laugh (at you), they'll bond (over you being clumsy), and they'll connect with each other—a recipe for good feelings. Socializing isn't only fun, it's also healthy for kids emotionally and intellectually. It promotes adult success, as they learn to navigate situations and value other people's opinions.

Experiences also make our kids more interesting, which furthers their social lives, seeing as people *like* interesting friends. Trampoline tales, rock-climbing escapades, even sagas of walking the dog have the power to entertain. Constant conversations about shopping, on the other hand, are less appealing to other people. How do I know? Another experiment from Van Boven. He paired up students and randomly assigned each to speak either about an experience that made them happy or a material good that brought them joy. Those who spoke about experiences were better liked by their partners.

See, we can't help but stamp a dollar value to material goods. Prices are relayed in numbers, a system devised entirely for the purpose of comparison. And if psychologists know *anything* about comparison, it's that when we measure ourselves—or our stuff—against others, we will be miserable. Material goods can also be disappointing when they fall short of our own comparisons, says Van Boven. Sometimes you buy something and it looks better in the store or online than at home. Sometimes you're certain your new hat will mesmerize your friends, but doesn't. When hats do not deliver the great promise we believed they would bring, we're disappointed. Experiences, on the other hand, might just be resistant to comparisons. Van Boven's work points to a

1998 study in which subjects were asked whether they'd rather earn $50,000 a year when others were earning $25,000 or earn $100,000 when others were earning $200,000 and most of them choose to earn more than everyone else, even though that meant making less money. But when it came to vacation time, no one cared what anyone else was doing. People took as much as they could get, regardless of how much their peers had.

Spending money also makes us happiest when we spend it on other people, according to research from Michael I. Norton, a business administration professor at Harvard University Business School, who performed a series of experiments that measured happiness levels before and after financial windfalls.[7] The happiest people in one study were those who spent a $20 windfall on someone they knew. The second happiest were those who turned it into a charitable donation, and the least happy people were those who spent the money on themselves.

How can we apply that at home without inadvertently implying it is okay to give all our money away? We can assign our kids the tasks of buying their friends' and siblings' birthday presents. We can require them to donate a portion of their allowance to the charity of their choice. And we can take them to buy school supplies for kids in shelters, and drop them off together.

When you are going to spend money on your kids in hopes of buying the occasional burst of joy—we're all going to do it at some point—we'll get more happiness from each dollar if we buy small stuff, such as chocolate, bubble bath, or movie admissions.[8] Dr. Richard Tunney of the University of Nottingham studied lottery winners and learned that it wasn't the flashy cars or expensive jewelry that made people happy. It was the simple purchases such as reading a book and enjoying a bottle of wine. When in his study Tunney looked at all people—even those that hadn't won the lottery—the happiest reported enjoying frequent, low-cost treats. The least happy people, meanwhile, were always rewarding themselves with purchases that never seemed to be satisfying.

Here's how it works with your hard-earned money, not lottery winnings. Say you're willing to spend $50 on spreading a little joy throughout your household. You could buy your kid a pair of purple Converse sneakers. If we were awarding happiness points on a scale of 1 to 10, perhaps the sneakers would provide 8 points. Done. But had you spent $5 on chocolate, she might get 3 points. Then in a few days, $15 on a T-shirt could get her another 5 points. Then a free movie-making app, 6 points. Then a new hair tie costing $4 could deliver 3 points. With small stuff, the kid already has double the happiness and $26 left.

What's more, each little burst of joy is likely to spill over to other areas of your kid's life. For example, a relaxing bubble bath may spark her creativity, and she could later draw a picture that brings her more happiness. She could use her movie app to showcase her friend's soccer skills, who might turn around with an invitation to a sleepover.

If we fear our kids are materialistic—and we've checked and double-checked the boxes for rewards and self-esteem—we may want to adjust their schedules. That's because kids with the perfect balance of free time and scheduled activities were the least materialistic, according to research from James Roberts, a marketing professor at Baylor University.[9] Turns out, affluence doesn't relate only to money, but also to time. Baylor surveyed thirteen hundred ninth- and tenth-grade students and found that those who perceived their schedules to be manageable, with a good mix of enriching activities and relaxing downtime, were the least materialistic and most likely to have fulfilling friendships. Most kids have absolutely no free time or too much free time—both bad situations, according to this research. Overscheduled kids are quick to buy things (sunglasses, clothes, sneakers) as a way to relieve stress. Kids who lounge around on afternoons and weekends fall prey to marketing ploys. They wander around malls. They put their energy toward acquiring things, not learning or doing them.

Here's the catch: There's no formula for what researchers consider the perfect number of free and scheduled hours. Determining whether a schedule is stressful is based on each child's perception, not her actual schedule. The good news is that we can help improve our kids' outlook. That's mostly done by giving them some control. My friend Liz requires her daughters to make their own appointments for the orthodontist, dentist, or doctors. She'll drive them there, but she wants them to organize their own lives after school, allotting time for lacrosse, social activities, and schoolwork. Her theory: How is *she* supposed to know when they have tests or projects due?

Clearly, if our kids seem to have too much or too little free time, we should try to tinker with their schedules. But if that's not possible and we need them in a daily after-school activity—thanks to the nine-to-five-thirty workday—we can give our kids choices over the classes they take. If we find those activities too expensive, and our kids are at home with empty hours, we can come up with our own. We can task our tech-savvy kids with designing a website, artistic ones with creating exhibits, movie-makers with producing a film, or a kid with any interest in charge of planning the next family outing.

Rock-Solid Money Move

Materialism can cause psychological bruises, but the financial scars can also be pretty ugly. Filling emotional needs with store-bought stuff can sabotage our credit scores over time and, in turn, suffocate our ability to pay for the things good parents really do need to buy. Don't bother taking a family vote on the matter; your kids right now might not mind missing out on important parenting purchases (like textbooks). But when it comes to college and cosigning their car loans, our teens—who will by then find us embarrassing enough—are gonna want parents with good credit.

Everyone is at risk for ruining his or her credit score, not only the weak and impulsive. In fact, those of us with the most willpower, diligently paying our bills on time *and in full,* are also most likely to accumulate the most debt after a few slip-ups, according to research from Keith Wilcox at Columbia Business School. It's called the "What the hell" effect, and it causes the strong-willed people to figure, after going about 3 percent over their credit limits, a few more charges won't hurt.[10]

They do.

Credit card interest has the evil power of turning a $50 sweater into a $351 sweater—*and it's the same sweater*. Here's how it works: If we put $50 on a credit card and make only minimum payments, that $50 will balloon to $351 after just one year of 18 percent interest every month ($50, $59, $69, $81, $95, $112, $132 . . . $298, $351.) The stupid sweater sits in our closets getting more boring while at the same time *getting more expensive*. (Evil!)

We have to make it stop. If we're carrying credit card balances over from month to month, we must stack up those bills by order of interest rate: the card charging the highest rate on top, the lowest on the bottom. We'll make monthly payments to all of them. But we'll tackle the total amount for the most expensive card—it has the highest rate of interest—first. Any time we find ourselves with extra money, we will remember how a seemingly innocent $50 purchase will transform into an ugly and massive debt hanging over our heads, following us everywhere. And we will know that putting our extra money toward the problem—not another purchase—will push it away.

We're also allowed to call our credit card companies. Behind those faceless statements with scary numbers and fine print are actual people who prefer to get paid. Some of them are even open to negotiations.

If we're committed to continued payments, we'll want to pull out the card with the lowest interest rate, because it's the cheapest card. Call that company and offer a deal: You'll move all your balances over to them—have the amount added up beforehand—if the company can lower the interest rate another 2 percentage points. We may get 1 point, we may get 1.5, we may get 0.5. But it's a lighter load. And for the card: It gets another bank's profits, seeing as you'll now be paying the company interest that was destined for a competitor.

When it comes to other debt, our mortgages and car loans are fine, assuming we pay them. That last part is pretty important. Those loans are "secured" in that they are fixed firmly to something—a car or a house—that the lender can take back if we don't pay.

If we can't pay our car loans, we're better off selling the damn cars and using the money to settle the debt. That's because, it turns out, vehicle repossession is pretty accurately portrayed in movies. They just come and take your car away, no notice required.[11] When taking out our car loans, most of us signed papers saying that we understand this. The repossession of a vehicle is unpleasant for many expensive reasons. For starters, by the time they come for your car, you've lost the chance to make monthly payments—they probably won't give it back unless you pay off the whole loan. And of course they'll tack on towing and storage costs. If you don't pay, they sell your car, though there is the tiny detail of it not being yours anymore.

Mortgage companies, it seems, are a little more sensitive. Either that, or even *they* don't want to deal with selling your house. Either way, if you fall behind, some lenders will temporarily reduce or suspend your payments. Others may reduce the amount you owe each month, but extend the life of the loan. Whatever happens, just know three credit agencies are keeping track of every financial move we make. Our credit reports, as we all know, are our financial profile maintained by the three agencies: Equifax (www.equifax.com), Experian (www.experian.com), and TransUnion (www.transunion.com).

There are lots of ways to keep our scores high. We can always pay our bills, even if it's the minimum payment. We shouldn't use more than 30 percent of available credit. And we've got to maintain a healthy mix of loans: mortgage, car, credit card, and store branded. If we apply for too many credit cards over, say, a one-month period, we look desperate, and even credit agencies find that unattractive.

Maybe you actually are desperate and thinking, *Hey, thanks, Brett, for the super obvious tips about paying my bills on time, but I'm about two years past that and about to hire a debt relief agency. That's* fine. But first check out the company with your state attorney general and local consumer protection agency. There are some reputable credit-counseling organizations that can help you to manage money. Most are nonprofits offered through universities, military bases, or credit unions. Then again, there are plenty of companies that pretend to help people get back on their feet financially who in reality are pulling the rug out from under their customers. Credit repair clinics, for example, will promise to clean up your credit history for a fee. But they can't do anything for you that you can't do for yourself, says the Federal Trade Commission.[12] You can correct inaccurate information in your file, but no one—regardless of what they say—can remove accurate negative information from your credit report. Only time and a conscientious effort to pay your debts can clean things up.

What's worse, your credit repair company can be fraudulent and can get you into trouble. If the company does any of the following, run:

- Insist you pay them before they do any work on your behalf
- Tell you not to contact the credit reporting companies directly
- Tell you to dispute information in your credit report that you know is accurate
- Tell you to give false information on your applications for credit or a loan
- Don't explain your legal rights when they tell you what they can do for you

Even more dangerous are companies promising a "new credit identity." Turns out, that's code for one of the two federal crimes they're about to push people into committing. Customers pay for the privilege of becoming their accomplices.

It may sound sanitizing to hear a company claim it can help you clean up your credit by hiding a bad history or a bankruptcy, but it's dirty work. These companies either sell you a stolen Social Security number—often pilfered from children, says the FTC—or they will provide you with a nine-digit number that looks like a social security number but call it a CPN (a credit profile number or credit privacy number). They may even tell you to apply to the IRS for an Employer Identification Number, which is legal—unless you happen to be using it to deceive banks or prospective employers. And when you are using a new CPN or EIN to hide your real credit history from people who are deciding whether to lend you money, then you are in violation of federal fraud laws. If you do commit criminal offenses, you're going to be in big legal trouble. And don't even think of telling the authorities, "But they *told* me to do it!" Because prosecutors will give you the same look we give our kids when one of them steals cookies and blames his brother. Except here, you're dealing with people who have the authority to send you to prison. (And they don't secretly think the whole crime is a little bit cute.)

Even our legal options for debt elimination come with a heaping side of risk. Debt settlement programs, for example, are offered by for-profit companies who tell you that, after negotiating with your creditors, they can get the credit card companies to happily accept much less than you actually owe, sometimes 30 to 60 percent of that amount, according to the FTC. You, in turn, agree to set aside a specific amount of money every month in savings, usually into an escrow-like account. This might make sense until you realize your creditors are under no obligation to lower your bills. So even if you do your part and set aside the money, you could wind up paying this debt management company for the privilege of simply paying your debts, as always. What's more, your debt manager usually starts with the smallest bills, meaning interest and fees on your massive debts will continue to grow, says the FTC.

These programs usually tell their clients to stop making any monthly payments to their creditors so the company can do its job— which can really work against you. First, it doesn't look good on your credit report. What's more, your debts will continue to accrue late fees and penalties that can put you further in the hole. The companies you owe are still going to call you (and call you and call you) requesting payment. Some might even sue you. If they win, they might be able to garnish your wages or put a lien on your home.

After all that, many people wind up dropping out of these programs anyway. Making the payments for thirty-six months (the average time) isn't always affordable. And even though you'll get that money back, you left behind a huge mess.

Don't Be Duped by a Debt Relief Company

Avoid any organization—whether it's credit counseling, debt settlement, or any other service—that does any of the following:

- Charges any fees before it settles your debts or enters you into a debt management plan (DMP)

- Pressures you to make "voluntary contributions," which is really another name for fees

- Touts a "new government program" to bail out personal credit card debt

- Guarantees it can make your unsecured debt go away

- Tells you to stop communicating with your creditors, but doesn't explain the serious consequences

- Tells you it can stop all debt collection calls and lawsuits

- Guarantees that your unsecured debts can be paid off for pennies on the dollar

- Won't send you free information about the services it provides without requiring you to provide personal financial information, like your credit card account numbers and balances

- Tries to enroll you in a debt relief program without reviewing your financial situation with you
- Offers to enroll you in a DMP without teaching you budgeting and money management skills
- Demands that you make payments into a DMP before your creditors have accepted you into the program

(Source: Federal Trade Commission)

CHAPTER NINE

Congratulations, Your Kid Got into a Great College

choose
PEACEFUL RETIREMENT
OVER PILES OF DEBT

Save Estimated $388,164

The Stuff You'll Skip

Campus Consultants Inc. predicts the average cost
of four years at a public, in-state university to be
$229,256, and four years at an Ivy League private col-
lege to cost $597,308, if tuition and fees rise 5 percent
by 2033, according to Kalman Chany.

The difference being $368,052. That's all I'll say. Few
of us will have the total amount of an Ivy League
school—$597,308—to invest for 18 years.

Clayton Thomas had a father with parenting skills that could make many of us feel inadequate. A lawyer with degrees from Yale University and Columbia University, Clayton's dad was raising the spelling bee champion who took calculus before it was even offered to other students his son's age. He enrolled Clayton in a Shakespearean writing class—seriously, most parents I know spend time figuring out how to cut down on driving to after-school activities, not in search of new destinations—and pre-college programs offered by the most elite institutions in the country, including Stanford University.

Sports? Of course there were sports. Clayton excelled at all sorts of athletics from his toddler to his teen years. T-ball, biking, soccer, skiing—the usuals and the exceptionals, involving helmets and lift tickets. "I can't say the writing classes didn't make me a better writer," says Clayton, now thirty years old. "And I still love to ski, thanks to being put on the slopes at a young age. But the objective was to help me, and it didn't work. It was such a loss of time and energy. That's what I really wish I had back more than anything. The time. Because the experience was such a drain. It wasn't satisfying or fulfilling. It was a grind."

But it paid off, most of us would point out, after hearing Clayton got an acceptance letter from Duke University. Off in Durham, North Carolina, he majored in biochemistry—just as his dad wished—and even got research jobs at esteemed labs with government funding. But at a critical juncture in the Clayton Thomas Lifetime Success Plan, things fell apart. Clayton was burned out. He couldn't bear the thought of applying to medical school to become the surgeon his father had been grooming. He was stepping off the path. He was going to find a job immediately after graduation. He would use his Ivy League degree. "My first disappointment of graduating from a top-ten school was not being able to find a job," he says. "What dawned on me after I graduated and got into the workforce was that no one cared where I had gone to school. I don't know if this was a reasonable expectation, but I did believe when I was a student at Duke that my degree would open a huge array of doors. And not just because of the name recognition. But because I would have gained something significant from that degree to make myself marketable."

Eventually, the pizza delivery job he did land wasn't covering rent, so Clayton returned to his mom's home in Salt Lake City. With his dad no longer calling to ask about medical school, it got quiet. Clayton could finally hear his calling: computers. Clayton enrolled in a two-year community college and got a degree in computer science. He got a job a week after graduation—that's seven days, for anyone keeping track—and was soon after that recruited by a top-level consulting company. Executives there flew him out to Chicago for an interview and immediately after hiring him—yay—sent Clayton to California for training. Next he traveled to Canada for his first assignment, then South Africa, and soon he was sharing his story with me on a phone call he placed from the United Kingdom, where he was working on a software platform for insurance companies. Or something. (It all sounds very complicated.)

"My community college degree landed me my dream job," says Clayton, pointing out that a semester cost $1,300 compared to $18,000 at Duke. "I'm traveling the world on an expense account. You could say that having Duke on my resume helped me get this job. But other people in my classes from community college are also working, some in positions more senior to mine. And I have a friend from Duke who was a computer science major and has a similar job. So then you have to ask, 'What's the point of spending all that time and money?' If I could do it again, I'd go to a state school. There, I would have graduated with better grades, I'd have a better social life, and I'd have $100,000 in the bank. What's more, I wouldn't have been so burned out at the end of it all. I would have better weathered any setbacks."

Clayton Thomas is a real person—I didn't even change his name or any details, like some of the other people throughout these pages—who illustrates the results of at least four separate research studies and some one hundred thousand subjects that in unison tell us we don't have to automatically and unquestionably shell out $250,000 so our kids can go to the most elite college accepting them. We can send them, for sure. Many of us will still want to. But we need to know that the imagined returns of a highly selective school—the CEO-size income, the grand social status, and the enormous life satisfaction—come with considerable risk. There's a chance that after paying $250,000 in tuition, our kids will wind up with none of those things. What's more, these days you can get anything for less money, and a lifetime of status and satisfaction is no exception. Smart and ambitious people with less prestigious degrees have been proven to achieve the same level of success as their Ivy League counterparts. As both Clayton and scientific research prove, sometimes your college major matters more than your alma mater. And even if your kid isn't an academic, scientists have found serious social factors that contribute to people leading rich lives—and we're speaking here strictly in the financial sense.

It's enough to make us carefully consider the price of our kids' college but never (I repeat: never) whether they go—the cost of *not* having a college degree is steepest of all. On virtually every measure of economic well-being and career attainment, from personal earnings to job satisfaction, young college graduates ages twenty-five to thirty-two years old outperform people the same age but with less education, says the Pew Research Center. They earn more money, are less likely to be unemployed, and are more likely to report their jobs are stepping-stones to greater careers. Their non-college-educated counterparts? They say their jobs are leading nowhere.

The question is which school our kids will attend. There is plenty of evidence proving that attending an elite university has a great economic return. See for yourself on PayScale.com, where you can find that MIT grads earned a median $126,000 while neighboring Massachusetts College of Liberal Arts grads clocked in at $55,100. Princeton grads by midcareer had median incomes of $113,900, while New Jersey City University grads earned an average of $73,100. And for one final example, Duke graduates—which might even include Clayton—earned a median $108,000, while the amount for Winston-Salem grads was $59,000.

But instead of just sitting there, letting the Ivy Leagues take credit for cultivating the world's highest-earning professionals, economists Alan B. Krueger and Stacy Berg Dale asked a really good question: Do people with fancy diplomas earn more money because their schools were so great? Or, or, *or* do these people earn more money because *they're* so great?[1] Born, perhaps, with the kind of intelligence and ambition that allows them to find solutions, produce results, navigate situations, and work well with colleagues? Basically the researchers asked: Would these people make good money no matter *where* they went to school?

The answer is yes. Yes, they would.

These economists looked at more than 14,239 exceptional students who graduated college in 1976. Many played on varsity teams, more than 40 percent of them were ranked in the top 10 percent of their classes, and all of them got over 1350 on the SAT exam (because in the olden days, 1600 was a perfect score). For every one of these people who attended the likes of Duke, Georgetown, Columbia, Stanford, and University of Pennsylvania, the researchers were able to find someone else who was accepted to those schools but instead chose a lower-ranking institution. Almost twenty years after graduation the researchers were able to see that there was no difference in earnings between people who enrolled in selective colleges and people who turned them down in favor of less selective ones.

But come on, this was 1976—a time so ancient viewers had to walk to the television to change its channels. So the researchers went back and did the same test again, this time with students entering college in 1989.[2] While they were at it, they revisited the 1976 people and looked at *their* earnings for an even longer time span. Once again, they found no real payoff in terms of earnings to attending a more selective school.

There was an exception: Elite schools really did boost earnings for kids coming from severely disadvantaged circumstances. You don't have to be an econometrician to predict that the incomes of poor students who graduate from dilapidated or dangerous schools, and begin anew at Ivy League campuses with high-achieving peers and career resource centers, will do much, much better than the kids who turned down those opportunities to stay in inner cities or remotely rural ones. For everyone else, more important to future earnings than where our kids go to school is the major they choose. I, for one, recharted my entire life's course after changing from a business concentration to one in economics, thanks to a four-second analysis from which I drew the following conclusions:

1. Economics is easier.
2. Economics and business are the same. Like, no one—my parents or prospective employers—would be able tell the difference. Right? (Because no one knows the minds of prospective employers like a nineteen-year-old who impulsively changes to an easier major.)
3. My boyfriend was an economics major.

So you can see I'd seriously considered all the circumstances. I was wrong on only one important front: Business and economics majors do not get the same jobs. And thanks to my econ degree, I got a position as a government economist calculating the most widely watched inflation indicators, discussing them on CNBC, and working alongside

Ivy League graduates. I became a reporter covering the economy, a columnist covering the economy, I became known as "The Home Economist" and trademarked the name, gaining a television segment and newspaper column of the same name. And I am writing a book based on all the economic studies I've read.

In case it wasn't immediately obvious—you know, with the government job and the state of the newspaper industry—this is a happy ending. Because regardless of what *you* think of a career as a government economist, I thought it was awesome. We even had a softball team.

So while that worked out, for me, the story was designed to illustrate that a person's college major makes a big difference. That's why I suggest (and probably Clayton would as well) that our kids put the time into choosing their majors. Economists at the Center for Labor Market Studies found that a student's major had much more of an impact on her earnings than the college from which she graduated. Basically, earning a computer science degree from a community college is more likely to reap high earnings than an art history degree from a fancy university.

Now, because my early college boyfriend Mark Moskowitz is not likely available to help all our kids choose majors, we should turn to Anthony P. Carnevale and his team of researchers at the Georgetown University Center on Education and the Workforce. They studied three million college graduates between ages twenty-five and sixty-four and discovered that while most majors weren't linked to a particular occupation (for example, 6 percent of nursing majors worked as managers), they could clearly pull out the majors most likely to earn people high paychecks.[3] The top-earning majors—STEM and business—could make $3.4 million more over a lifetime than lower-paying majors. Bachelor's degrees in some majors earned more money than graduate degrees in others.

If you want to make a lot of money, choose engineering. Engineering majors, particularly petroleum engineers, made the most money. Counseling psychology and early childhood education, human services, and social work are the lowest-paying occupations.

Engineer Your Way to Higher Wages with These College Majors

Major	Median Annual Wages of College-Educated Workers Ages 25–29
Petroleum engineering	$136,000
Sciences and admin	$113,000
Metallurgical engineering	$97,000
Mining and mineral engineering	$97,000
Chemical engineering	$96,000
Electrical engineering	$93,000
Aerospace engineering	$90,000
Mechanical engineering	$87,000
Computer engineering	$87,000
Geological and geophysical engineering	$87,000
Computer science	$83,000
Civil engineering	$83,000
Applied mathematics	$83,000
Engineering	$81,000
Physics	$81,000

(Source: Georgetown Center on Education and the Workforce, "What's It Worth? The Economic Value of College Majors." from Georgetown University Table 2.1)

If helping other people doesn't pay off in the job market, *being liked* by them most certainly can increase a person's earnings. Researchers from University of Illinois found a clear link between popularity and earnings—meaning the kids with lots of friends in high school made more money as adults.[4] The high earners weren't necessarily the *coolest* kids, mind you. They were the kids who were very well liked, which typically requires possessing the kind of warm personalities most of us admire. These researchers followed a diverse group of eleven thousand tenth-grade students, and they asked the kids to name their three best friends. Students who got the most nominations were considered most popular. They also tracked test scores, teacher appraisals, and participation in extracurricular activities. Ten years later, they contacted the kids again and got their reported income and found that extra friend nomination turned into a 2 percent increase in income. They found a 10 percent difference in incomes between some of the least and most popular students. Motivational skills mattered as much as test scores. Kids whose teachers consider them to be conscientious, cooperative, and motivated were also high-earning. These were the kids who would work hard for good grades, complete assignments, and arrive on time to class.

The link between likeability and high earnings shows that if we (by "we" I mean the United States of America) are trying to raise kids who can earn respectable salaries, we should focus on more than cognitive skills, says Christy Lleras, an assistant professor at University of Illinois. "It's important to note that good schools do more than teach reading, writing, and math," says Lleras. "They socialize students."

You know what else? Smart people may make more money, as studies have been proving for years, but they don't necessarily build up more wealth, according to Jay Zagorsky, author of the study and a research scientist at Ohio State University.[5] He followed 7,403 Americans around for years and figured out that people of below-average intelligence were about as wealthy as those in similar circumstances but with higher IQs. The smarter ones may have gotten paid more, but many of them weren't able to save money and some got into big financial trouble. In fact, more people with high IQs had maxed out credit cards than people with low IQs. "People don't become rich just because they are smart," says Zagorsky. "Your IQ has no relationship to your wealth. Financial success means more than just income. You need to build up wealth to buffer life's storms and prepare for retirement."

The bottom line is that our goal in sending our kids to college is to arm them to thrive in the real world. But their futures depend on much more than the rank of the institution issuing their diplomas. If you decide to pay for an expensive college, be real about your reasons. We have all encountered people with Ivy League degrees who are virtually unemployable. Sometimes they get really good jobs but later lose them, regardless of their impressive test scores and diplomas. You don't find these people in large numbers, but you do raise an eyebrow when you hear their credentials. The tragic outcome for too many innocent bystanders is that they become overly active in the school's PTA. Perhaps *that's* where we need stricter admissions criteria.

Raise Them Better for Less

There are four ways to spend less money on your kid's college education.

1. Choose a less expensive college.
2. Get grants.
3. Get scholarships
4. Have your child pay for her *own* college with loans.

If you happen to be reading the last chapter of a book on why it's unnecessary to buy organic mattresses while learning that teens manage to succeed without personal soccer coaches, then option 2, Pell Grants from the government, may not be available to you. Those don't have to be repaid but are reserved for low-income students. Many elite schools —and all the Ivy League institutions—have "no-loan" financial aid policies that reduce tuition costs to a price similar to public colleges for kids who qualify. But they typically follow Pell Grant guidelines when it comes to qualifying kids.

Scholarships are also free money, but they're awarded on merit. Because each of us truly believes our child is exceptional and deserving of national recognition, scholarship scams are very common. There are tons of red flags. If a program charges an application fee, that's your first signal of a scam, says Mark Kantrowitz, senior vice president and publisher of Edvisors.com. If your child is awarded a scholarship for which she did not apply, it is unlikely that she is shining so brightly even those in the distance can see. It is likely a scam even—or especially—if they also sent a check. Take a look at the back, says Kantrowitz, because there's probably some fine print declaring your cashing that baby means you don't mind those people making monthly deductions from your checking account. Even seemingly big organizations are in on the game. If you hear from a trustworthy nonprofit dedicated to making the world a better place, check IRS Publication 78, says Kantrowitz. It's just a Google search away, and you can see whether the organization is registered with the government. If you're invited to a free informational seminar where you're told not to trust your overworked school guidance counselor, it's the seminar organizers who are likely dishonest.

Even if you do get a legitimate scholarship, it probably won't cover the full cost of college. Many of them are one-time payments that can range between $1,000 and even $25,000. At a school costing $60,000 a year, you've got fewer than six months covered.

So then there are loans. Average student debt is about $33,000 upon graduation, by Kantrowitz's calculations, and judging by the statistics, that kind of debt could be incurred by any one of our kids. Of course students across the economic board borrow tuition money— some 69 percent of graduates have debt—but those with the most educated parents heading the most affluent families now make up the biggest increases in borrowing, says Pew Research Center.

The pesky thing about student loans is that they have to be repaid—with interest. That's one of those statements you read and think, *What kind of a finance book is this?* Loans have to be repaid? *With interest?* Truly you are a scholar of economics imparting upon us some great economic wisdom, no? But there are some side effects of student debt that are just now surfacing.

If our kids take out loans, we'd better bask in their awesome educations now—buy a few sweatshirts from the bookstore for sure—because it could be a long time before we're bragging about grandchildren. College graduates saddled with student debt tend to delay life events, such as having children. For the first time in ten years, people who are thirty years old and have debt are actually less likely than people their age without debt to get mortgages, according to data from the Federal Reserve Board of New York.[6] Meaning, unless you happen to be a thirty-year-old with some $150,000 in cash, you're not buying a home.

It's become so common for adult kids (you know what I mean) to move back home with their parents that economists had to come up with a name for the phenomenon: boomeranging. (They did a good job with that one, particularly if you consider what they named some of those economic indicators . . .) More than 90 percent of millennials (kids born after 1980) left home at age twenty-one but more than 54 percent of them came back, according to the Bureau of Labor Statistics. It's not a huge shock to learn that kids from the wealthiest families—most likely with extra bedrooms and top-of-the-line appliances—were most likely to return to their parents' houses before the age of twenty-seven. Those with bachelor's degrees were more likely to come home than high school dropouts.

If the thought of your baby coming home again fills your heart with joy, keep in mind: She'll probably also want to borrow your car. Throughout the history of auto loans, people with student debt are more likely to finance a car—the college education made them richer. Until now. There has been a steep drop in the number of people with student loan debt who also borrowed money to buy a car, says the NY Fed.

What's going on? Well, the job market has presented its share of gloom, so when people expect to make less money, they tend to spend less money. But guess what else? It's hard for people with student loans to get approved for credit. Lenders have tightened standards, and it's not unheard of for grads to miss a few payments, thanks to either complicated repayment instructions or a lack of incoming funds. In 2012, credit scores for twenty-five-year-olds with student debt were 15 points lower than those without debt, says the NY Fed. For thirty-year-olds, the difference was 24 points.

People with student debt are better educated and tend to have higher incomes—you know, from all the education. But US households headed by adults under age forty with some debt have seven times less the net worth of the similar households headed by an adult without debt, according to Pew Research Center. Young adults who took out loans to finance their educations were less satisfied overall with their personal financial situations than those who did not borrow money, it found. They are likely to delay getting married and starting families.

While we won't want to borrow to our (kids') brains' content, loans can still be a helpful way to finance an education. And we can even minimize the delay in getting grandchildren or retiring by following this rule of thumb: Student debt at graduation should be less than the student's annual starting salary and, if you can swing it, a lot less, says Kantrowitz. That way, repayment is possible in ten years. If you can do it sooner, you'll save a lot of money in interest.

Same goes for us. If we're borrowing on our kids' behalf, we shouldn't borrow more than we can afford to repay in ten years or by retirement—whichever comes first. Meaning if retirement is only five years away, Kantrowitz recommends we borrow only half as much. (Find salary estimates for specific jobs at www.bls.gov/ooh.)

There are two kinds of student loans: federal loans (from the government) and private loans (from a bank). Both are loans we repay with interest, but the government ones—at least for students—tend to come with lower interest rates. They also offer payment plans that are based on our kids' incomes. And have protections if you defer or postpone payments, say, if you lose your job.

Private loans, on the other hand, might offer lower interest rates for parents with excellent credit. In some cases, if we don't need the deferment plans, or the federal government's other leniencies, it might be cheaper to refinance to a private loan. We just have to compare the costs.

We really want to be careful about how much money we borrow. For starters, we're dealing here with the federal government, an organization that is not kidding around when it comes to money. If you miss payments, the government can garnish your wages, prevent you from renewing a professional license, and intercept your tax refund, says Kantrowitz. They're happy to alert your credit agencies, which will put this on your credit report, which in turn could prevent you from renting an apartment or getting a mortgage.

Payments begin upon graduation. And one day after missing a payment, the borrower becomes delinquent. These loans do not disappear if you file for bankruptcy. They do not evaporate if you retire: The government will simply help itself to 15 percent of your Social Security check.

Maybe that's why they're not too worried about letting you borrow as much as you want. The Direct PLUS Loan program is for parents of dependent undergraduate students, and while you'll need good credit (being bankruptcy-free and foreclosure-less is helpful), your income and other expenses don't matter, says Kantrowitz. Basically you can make tons of money, use it to finance your yacht, and still borrow from this program. The first step in getting a student loan is filling out the FAFSA (Free Application for Federal Student Aid). You get an application at FAFSA.ed.gov. The forms come out on January 1 for the following school year (for example, on January 1, 2020, the forms will be published for the 2020–21 school year). Get them as soon as possible because some options, such as state and institutional grants and work-study opportunities, are disbursed on a first-come, first-served basis.

Fill out the form. Period. We don't get financial aid without it, and chances are—with four years at a public college slated to cost $229,256 in 2033—we're going to need to borrow a few bucks. Colleges and universities, Kantrowitz swears, don't hold it against your kid for applying. But they aren't likely to jump in to help in his sophomore or junior year, either, unless you can show your situation has drastically changed. If you can't prove you've lost your job or have had to pay your sister's living expenses, and you can't pay for college, your kid can't go. Dropout city.

Rock-Solid Money Move

Thinking about retirement savings is so much more boring than thinking about earning $100 million by inventing something really cool and never having to worry about money again. But when it comes to our inventions, we have to manufacture prototypes and develop marketing plans and *even* after all that we *still* have to worry about retirement.

By the time we are of Golden Girl age, Social Security and Medicare—the two government programs in place to support old people—could be as over as that sitcom about four women living in Florida (except that you won't be able to relive it all on DVD). The trustees of the Social Security tucked inside their last report a note to the public saying that at this rate, neither program can sustain long-run costs. Social Security expenditures have exceeded income, they write, while also tossing about the words *face depletion*.[7] So yeah, we might want to have a few dollars saved while we invent a zero-calorie wine or write our screenplays or decide that ripped tube socks are the next big thing. But to battle any boredom at the idea of saving for retirement, we can tweak the way we think. Basically, the whole idea will be more enjoyable if instead of focusing on boring bank accounts named with acronyms, we think specifically about the picturesque days we're trying to fund, according to research from Sean McCrea, a professor of psychology at the University of Wyoming.

Successful savings—or successful anything, really—is about motivating ourselves. It's much more exciting to sock away money for long days on the lake fishing or sunset walks on the beach than it is to focus only on an account named for a section of the IRS code.

If you think about it, saving for retirement is a lot like funding a second childhood. Along with free time for fishing and the comeback of diapers, retirement also is a time to once again mark our half birthdays. These are very important when it comes to our benefits. For example, when you turn fify-nine and a half, you can start withdrawing funds from your retirement accounts. And when you turn seventy and a half, you absolutely must start taking money from your traditional IRA.

So how much do you need to sock away right now? Figure that out on the ChooseToSave.org calculator. After that, there's no investment advice here and if you happen to find some, please don't take it. I'm not qualified to recommend specific accounts for specific situations in this forum. That would be true even if I did have any idea about your personal financial situation, which—given my lack of magical powers—I do not. But I will go over a few of the retirement account options and their benefits, so we can all be fluent when stuffing them with funds. Keep in mind, any contribution or income limits mentioned here can change with the whims—or rather carefully thought-out considerations—of our Congress.

IRAs and Roth IRAs are individual retirement accounts that you open with a bank or brokerage accounts. Both IRAs will offer certain though distinct tax benefits, but for both, it's you who decides how the money is invested: stocks, bonds—take your pick. If you choose a traditional IRA, you can also select annuities (insurance investments that pay income).

There are a few differences in the two, but if you're any kind of rich—married and earning over $191,000 or single with an income of $129,000—don't bother learning them. You can't open a Roth IRA. (In case you were wondering—because I was—the *Roth* comes from Senator William Roth from Delaware, who sponsored the legislation.)

The biggest difference between these two IRAs is when we pay taxes on the money. With traditional IRAs, we pay taxes when we retire. For now, we can deduct the contribution amounts from our taxable incomes, and that lowers the amount we'll owe the government that year. But when we retire and begin to make withdrawals at age fifty-nine and a half, we pay taxes on that money. When funding Roth IRAs, we pay the taxes today. We don't get tax deductions but we also don't have to pay taxes in retirement, when we make withdrawals.

The decision comes down to this: Is our tax rate higher today than it will be when we're almost sixty years old? Find other differences below.

Traditional and Roth IRAs

Traditional and Roth IRAs allow you to save money for retirement. This chart highlights some of their similarities and differences.

Who can contribute?

Traditional: You can contribute if you (or your spouse if filing jointly) have taxable compensation, but not after you are age 70.5 or older.

Roth: You can contribute at any age if you (or your spouse if filing jointly) have taxable compensation and your modified adjusted gross income is below certain amounts.

Are my contributions deductible?

Traditional: You can deduct your contributions if you qualify.

Roth: Your contributions aren't deductible.

How much can I contribute?

The most you can contribute to *all* of your traditional and Roth IRAs is the smaller of:

• $5,500 (for 2014 and 2015), or $6,500 if you're age 50 or older by the end of the year

• your taxable compensation for the year

What is the deadline to make contributions?

Your tax return filing deadline (not including extensions). For example, you have until April 15, 2016, to make your 2015 contribution.

When can I withdraw money?

You can withdraw money anytime.

Do I have to take required minimum distributions?

Traditional: You must start taking distributions by April 1 following the year in which you turn age 70 1/2 and by December 31 of later years.

Roth: Not required if you are the original owner.

Are my withdrawals and distributions taxable?

Traditional: Any deductible contributions and earnings you withdraw or that are distributed from your traditional IRA are taxable. Also, if you are under age 59 1/2, you may have to pay an additional 10% tax for early withdrawals unless you qualify for an exception.

Roth: No, if it's a qualified distribution (or a withdrawal that is a qualified distribution). Otherwise, part of the distribution or withdrawal may be taxable. If you are under age 59 1/2, you may also have to pay an additional 10% tax for early withdrawals unless you qualify for an exception.

(Source: Internal Revenue Service)

A SIMPLE (Savings Incentive Match Plan for Employees) is an IRA that some small businesses (under one hundred people) can offer their employees. With these accounts, the company makes contributions to each employee's traditional IRA. (Nice.) Companies can choose one of two options: (1) Announce that for any contributions an employee makes to the account, the company will make a matching contribution—as long as it's not greater than 3 percent of the person's salary. Or (2) announce that the company will contribute 2 percent of each person's compensation to his or her retirement accounts, regardless of whether (or how much money) the employee contributes. As in all cases of free money, this is usually a very good thing.

A Simplified Employee Pension plan—a SEP IRA—is a traditional IRA suitable for a business of any size, including a one-person show. In these accounts, only employers—the company—can make contributions. But they can be big, up to 25 percent of each person's pay. The employer is, however, allowed to put restrictions on who gets the money. It can be reserved for only those over age twenty-one, or those who have worked for the company for three years, and received at least $650 in compensation from the employer. The company can reduce the restrictions (for example, making the minimum work time two years or six months) or eliminate them altogether. But it can't make it more difficult than that to get the contributions.

A payroll deduction IRA can be a traditional or a Roth account that is set up by the employee with a financial institution of her or his choice. The employee authorizes a certain amount to be deducted from her paycheck, and the company then puts it directly into the account.

A 401(K) is also for retirement, but they're called profit-sharing plans because the company can put a portion of its profits toward employee retirement. We—assuming we're the employees in this situation—authorize a portion of our paychecks as contributions, and we won't have to pay taxes on that money. (Yet.) The employer can match our contributions or decide on another amount.

We'll own our contributions from the moment we make them, but with traditional plans, the company's contributions can be vested, meaning we might have to work there a certain amount of time before they are officially ours. Other incarnations of these accounts, such as a Safe Harbor plan or a SIMPLE 401(k) plan, are vested immediately.

With these plans, we'll select from a menu of investment options. Choices will probably include mutual funds of stocks, bonds, or a combination. Sometimes it will be an aggressive mix of securities that will grow more conservative as we age.

If you change jobs, it's important to be well versed on the idea of rolling over your retirement plan.

1. For starters, there's a deadline: We only have only sixty days from the time we get the money to roll it over.
2. If we miss the deadline, we lose 10 percent of the money to taxes.

Basically, rolling over your plan from one account to a new account involves asking your plan administrator or the financial institution holding the account to send that money to a new account. Or you can do it yourself.

Good luck to us all and see you in the adult living community— where hopefully we'll each have loads of savings and lots of sanity.

Let's hope our kids come visit.

Acknowledgments

This book is a culmination of my many professional endeavors, including those in economics, print reporting, magazine writing, online articles, and television news. All those opportunities were possible because, in each case, a very important person who didn't have to take my phone call took it anyway. Every one of these people has since evolved in their own careers, but in thanking them here I include their professional affiliations at the time and offer my sincere gratitude to Darlene Williams from the Bureau of Labor Statistics, Susan Postlewaite from the Miami *Daily Business Review*, Carol Brooks from *Glamour* magazine, Rodney Ward from *Nightly Business Report*, and Lisa Gibbs from the *Miami Herald*. Special thanks to Jacqueline Bueno Sousa and Anna Winderbaum, two people who were assigned to oversee me but ended up becoming dear friends. And to Susan Isaacs—yes, the famous mystery writer—who manages to sound genuinely interested in my progress as an author every time I interrupt her dinner.

I am lucky enough to count as my friends some of the most dynamic and beautiful people in the world. They live throughout

Miami, Key Biscayne, Boca Raton, Orlando, Miami Beach, New York, New Jersey, Boston, Los Angeles, Maine, and Washington, DC. You know who you are. Thank you for all your friendship over the years. I know it's not always easy but I hope you'll agree it's usually so much fun.

Thanks to Dr. Gwen Wurm for helping me decide American parents (but mostly us) needed the information included in this book. Gwen, as a doctor you are articulate and hilarious. As a friend, you are truly a gift. As a drinker, you could use some work.

To all the professors, scientists, and researchers who produced extraordinary findings, you are changing the world. I'm so grateful for your work, and also for taking my calls or answering my emails.

Nena Madonia from Dupree Miller, you have believed in me since the day you opened my Fed Ex envelope. I knew from our first conversation that I was in the hands of the savviest and smartest literary agent around. I couldn't wait to work with you then and I'm even more in awe of you now.

Stephanie Knapp, you are the editor extraordinaire. Thank you for encouraging my voice and my message. I would write an entire second book just to work with you again.

Mom and Dad, thanks for everything you've given me, but especially the tennis lessons and the college education. Both of those things have really come in handy. You're right, Mom, the older I get, the smarter you get. I love you both very much.

Darren, you've always been the world's greatest brother, but that's particularly true since you married Christine. I'm still not sure why Mom and Dad like you so much better than me. But at least we can laugh about it. And so much more.

Bob, I could not have teamed up with a better, or more handsome, partner in life. Your love, your support, and your ability to cook chili are just a few of the reasons I'm the luckiest, happiest, and most grateful woman in the world. I know for certain we'll be together for all of eternity. And yet never agree on the state of the leftover food in the refrigerator.

To Daelyn and Mica, together you are the greatest of all life's blessings. Being with you both—laughing, sharing, and cuddling—brings me love and light. Looking at you takes my breath away. And being your mother is a privilege and a pleasure. I'm sorry I dedicated so much time to writing a book about why it's bad to buy you more stuff.

Notes

INTRODUCTION

1. "Stock Investors Should Expect 6%–7% Annual Return, Buffet Says," *Bloomberg*, May 3, 2015, www.bloomberg.com/apps/news?pid=newsarchive&sid=a1. neDMy8DEU.
2. Frank Furstenberg and Sabino Kornrich, "Investing in Children: Changes in Parental Spending on Children, 1972–2007," *Demography* (September 2012) doi: 10.1007/s13524-012-0146-4, http://journalistsresource.org/studies/economics/inequality/investing-children-changes-parental-spending-children
3. Kalman A. Chany, *Paying for College Without Going Broke, 2015 Edition (College Admissions Guides)* (Natick, MA: Princeton Review, 2015).
4. Yongling Tu, "Toy Related Deaths and Injuries" 2012, Consumer Product Safety Commission (November 2013).
5. Jean M. Twenge, PhD, *Generation Me: Why Today's Young Americans Are More Confident, Assertive, Entitled—and More Miserable Than Ever Before* (New York: Atria Books, 2014).

CHAPTER 1

1. "Online Baby Product Sales in the US," Report OD5695, IbisWorld.com (July 2014).
2. "Durable Baby Goods Stores in the US," Report OD4386, IbisWorld.com (August 2013).
3. "Ethan Allen Recalls to Repair Drop-Side Cribs Due to Entrapment, Suffocation and Fall Hazards," Recall 11018, Consumer Product Safety Commission (October 22, 2010).

4. "Pottery Barn Kids Recalls to Repair Drop-Side Cribs Due to Entrapment, Suffocation and Fall Hazards," Release #10-302, Consumer Product Safety Commission (July 14, 2010).

5. "Bexco Recalls Franklin & Ben Mason 4-in-1 Convertible Cribs Due to Fall and Entrapment Hazards," Recall 14-258, Consumer Product Safety Commission (August 19, 2014).

6. "Oeuf Recalls to Repair Cribs Due to Entrapment Hazard," Recall 14-236, Consumer Product Safety Commission (July 22, 2014).

7. Amy Wagner, "FOX19 Investigates: Hacker hijacks baby monitor," Fox 19 Now, posted April 22, 2014, www.fox19.com/story/25310628/hacked-baby-monitor.

8. Cindy E. Rodriguez, "Baby Video Monitors Could Invite Burglars," ABCNews, posted October 29, 2010, http://abcnews.go.com/Technology/baby-video-monitors-invite-burglars/story?id=11992731.

9. "Two Strangulation Deaths Prompt Summer Infant to Recall Video Baby Monitors with Cords; Firm to Provide New On-Product Label & Instructions," Release #11-127, Consumer Product Safety Commission (February 11, 2011).

10. "Angelcare Recalls to Repair Movement and Sound Baby Monitors After Two Deaths Due to Strangulation Hazard," Recall 14-028, Consumer Product Safety Commission (November 21, 2013).

11. "Chelsea & Scott Recalls Idea Baby Bath Seats Due to Drowning Hazard; Sold Exclusively at Onestepahead.com," Recall #13-219, Consumer Product Safety Commission (June 18, 2013).

12. "Dream On Me Recalls Bath Seats Due to Drowning Hazard," Recall 13-061, Consumer Product Safety Commission (December 6, 2012).

13. "Thermobaby Bath Seats Recalled by SCS Direct Due to Drowning Hazard; Sold Exclusively at Amazon.com," Recall #13-240, Consumer Product Safety Commission (July 17, 2013).

14. Kevin Gipson, "Submersions Related to Non-Pool and Non-Spa Products, 2012 Report," Consumer Product Safety Commission (September 2012).

15. "Child Passenger Safety: Get the Facts," Center for Disease Control and Prevention (September 12, 2014).

16. You can find ratings for ease of use here: www.safercar.gov/parents/CarSeats/Car-Seat-Ratings-Ease-Of-Use.htm

17. "Child Passenger Safety: Get the Facts," Center for Disease Control and Prevention (September 12, 2014).

18. "Car Seats: Information for Families 2015," American Academy of Pediatrics, www.healthychildren.org/English/safety-prevention/on-the-go/Pages/Car-Safety-Seats-Information-for-Families.aspx.

19. "Benefits of Breastfeeding," Natural Resource Defense Council, www.nrdc.org/breastmilk/benefits.asp.

20. "Infant formula: Your questions answered," Mayo Clinic, January 19, 2013, www.mayoclinic.org/healthy-lifestyle/infant-and-toddler-health/in-depth/infant-formula/art-20045782.

21. Kelly Kiyeon Lee and Min Zhao, "The Effect of Price on Preference Consistency Over Time," *Journal of Consumer Research 41*, no. 1 (June 2014).

22. B. Hart and T. R. Risley, "The Early Catastrophe, The 30 Million Word Gap by Age 3" *Education Review 77*, no. 1 (2004): 100–118.

23. Heather Bortfeld, James L. Morgan, Roberta Michnick Golinkoff, and Karen Rathbun, "Familiar Names Help Launch Babies Into Speech-Stream Segmentation," *Psychological Science* 16, no. 4 (May 2005): 298–304.

24. Ari Brown, MD, "Media Use by Children Younger Than Two Years," American Academy of Pediatrics Policy Statement, *Pediatrics* 128, no. 5 (November 1, 2011).

25. Study of Hazardous Products in Thrift Stores, Consumer Product Safety Commission, www.cpsc.gov/en/Business--Manufacturing/Business-Education/ResaleThrift-Stores-Information-Center/.

26. Reebok Recalls Bracelet Linked to Child's Lead Poisoning Death, Release 06-119, Consumer Product Safety Commission (March 23, 2006).

27. Total Lead Content, Consumer Product Safety Commission, www.cpsc.gov/en/Business--Manufacturing/Business-Education/Lead/Total-Lead-Content/.

28. Sandy Baum, Jennifer Ma, and Kathleen Payea, Education Pays 2013: The Benefits of Higher Education for Individuals and Society, The College Board (2013).

CHAPTER 2

1. Campaign for a Commercial-Free Childhood, "Complaint and Request for Investigation and Relief in the Matter of Your Baby Can LLC and Dr. Robert Titzer," before the Federal Trade Commission, Washington DC 20554 (April 12, 2011).

2. "Ads Touting "Your Baby Can Read" Were Deceptive," FTC Complaint Alleges, FTC File No. 1123045, Federal Trade Commission (August 28, 2012).

3. Richard Perez-Pena, "Best, Brightest and Rejected: Elite Colleges Turn Away up to 95 Percent," *New York Times*, April 8, 2014.

4. Ari Brown, MD, "Media Use by Children Younger Than Two Years," American Academy of Pediatrics Policy Statement, *Pediatrics* 128, no. 5 (November 1, 2011): 1040 –45 (doi: 10.1542/peds.2011-1753).

5. Campaign for a Commercial-Free Childhood, "Request for Investigation of Deceptive Practices in Connection with Fisher-Price, Developer and Marketer of Mobile Apps for Infants and Very Young Children," Before the Federal Trade Commission, Washington DC, 20580, (August 7, 2013).

6. Letter from Mary K. Engle, associate director of the Federal Trade Commission, to Eric G. Null of Georgetown University Law Center and Susan Linn, EdD, of the Campaign for a Commercial-Free Childhood, March 31, 2014.

7. Richard Alleyne, "Playing a Musical Instrument Makes You Brainier," *The Telegraph*, October 27, 2009.

8. Tamar Lewin, "No Einstein in Your Crib? Get a Refund," *New York Times*, October 24, 2009.

9. Federal Trade Commission, "Company That Touted Products' Ability to Treat Children's Speech Disorders Settles FTC Charges It Deceived Customers," January 9, 2015.

10. Harnam Singh, PhD, and Michael W. O'Boyle, PhD, "Interhemispheric Interaction During Global-Local Processing in Mathematically Gifted Adolescents, Average-Ability Youth, and College Students," Australia; *Neuropsychology* 18, no. 2 2004: 371–77.

11. Alex Davidson, "Remedial Math," Forbes, March 2, 2009.

12. From the Kumon website, www.kumon.com.

13. Testimony of Kenneth Ginsburg, MD, MS, Ed, FAAP, on behalf of the American Academy of Pediatrics, "No Child Left Inside: Recconnecting Kids with the Outdoors," to the Natural Resources Subcommittee on National Parks, Forests and Public Lands and Subcommittee on Fisheries, Wildlife and Oceans (May 24, 2006).

14. O. Ybarra, P. Winkielman, I. Yeh, E. Burnstein, and L. Kavanagh, "Friends (and Sometimes Enemies) with Cognitive Benefits: What Types of Social Interactions Boost Executive Functioning" *Social Psychological and Personality Science* 2010: 10.1177/1948550610386808.

15. Brian N. Verdine, Roberta M. Golinkoff, Kathryn Hirsh-Pasek, Nora S. Newcombe, Andrew T. Filipowicz, and Alicia Chang, "Deconstructing Building Blocks: Preschoolers' Spatial Assembly Performance Relates to Early Mathematical Skills," *Child Development* (September 2013) doi: 10.1111/cdev.12165.

16. Susan C. Levine, Kristin R. Ratliff, Janellen Huttenlocher, and Joanna Cannon, "Early Puzzle Play: A Predictor of Preschoolers' Spatial Transformation Skill," October 31, 2011 doi: 10.1111/cdev.12165.

17. Cristine Legare and Tania Lombrozo, "Selective Effects of Explanation on Learning in Early Childhood," *Journal of Experimental Child Psychology* April 2014.

18. "Insurance Fraud," Federal Bureau of Investigation, www.fbi.gov/stats-services/publications/insurance-fraud.

19. "Chances of Disability," Council for Disability Awareness, www.disabilitycan-happen.org/chances_disability.

CHAPTER 3

1. Pam Bennett, "The Aftermath of the Great Recession: Financially Fragile Families and How Professionals Can Help," The Forum for Family and Consumer Issues, http://ncsu.edu/ffci/publications/2012/v17-n1-2012-spring/bennett.php.

2. "Expenditures on Children By Families," United States Department of Agriculture August 2014.

3. "Characteristics of New Housing," US Census Bureau, last revised June 1, 2015.

4. L. Chaddock-Heyman, C. H. Hillman, N. J. Cohen, and A. F. Kramer, "The Importance of Physical Activity and Aerobic Fitness for Cognitive Control and Memory in Children," *Monographs of the Society for Research in Child Development* 79, no. 4, 2014: 25–50.

5. Andrea Faber Taylor and Frances E. Kuo, "Children With Attention Deficits Concentrate Better After Walk in the Park," *Journal of Attention Disorders* August 25, 2008: doi:10.1177/1087054708323000

6. Niels Egelund, "The Mass Experiment 2012," a Danish experiment, Aarhus University.

7. Gary Evans and Richard Wener, "Angst and the Rail Commuter: Longer the Trip, Greater the Stress," *ScienceDaily* August 7, 2006 www.sciencedaily.com/releases/2006/08/060805124750.htm.

8. Erika Sandow, "Long-Distance Commuters Get Divorced More Often, Swedish Study Finds," *ScienceDaily* May 25, 2011 www.sciencedaily.com/releases/2011/05/110525085920.htm.

9. Marla E. Eisenberg, ScD, MPH; Rachel E. Olson, MS; Dianne Neumark-Sztainer, PhD, MPH, RD; Mary Story, PhD, RD; and Linda H. Bearinger, PhD, MS, JAMA; "Correlations Between Family Meals and Psychosocial Well-Being among Adolescents," Archives of Pediatrics and Adolescent Medicine, *Pediatrics* 158, no. 8 August 1, 2004.

10. Residential Energy Consumption Survey, Table CE2.6: "Household Fuel Expenditures in the US, Totals and Averages, 2009," Energy Information Administration, www.eia.gov/consumption/residential/data/2009/index.cfm?view=consumption#fuel-consumption.

11. Learn more about the Energy Star program at www.energystar.gov.

12. Print out a Mortgage Shopping Worksheet at www.consumer.ftc.gov/articles/pdf-0104-mortgage-shopping-worksheet.pdf.

CHAPTER 4

1. "Charter School Enrollment," National Center for Education Statistics, last updated April 2015, https://nces.ed.gov/programs/coe/indicator_cgb.asp.

2. Christopher Lubienski and Sarah Theule Lubienski, "Charter, Private, Public Schools and Academic Achievement, New Evidence from NAEP Mathmatics Data," January 2006, National Center for the Study of Privatization in Education, Columbia University."

3. Christopher A. Lubienski and Sarah Theule Lubienski, *The Public School Advantage: Why Public Schools Outperform Private Schools* (Chicago: University of Chicago Press: 2013).

4. Harold Wenglinsky, "Are Private High Schools Better Academically Than Public High Schools?" Center on Education Policy, October 10, 2007, www.cep-dc.org/displayDocument.cfm?DocumentID=121..

5. Paul E. Peterson and Elena Llaudet, "On the Public-Private School Achievement Debate," Harvard University, PEPG 06-02, Executive Summary.

6. Wenglinsky, "Private High Schools"

7. Caroline M. Hoxby, "The Effects of Class Size on Student Achievement: New Evidence from Population Variation," *Quarterly Journal of Economics* 115, no. 4 2000.

8. Table 208.20: "Public and Private Elementary and Secondary Teachers, Enrollment, Pupil/Teacher Ratios, and New Teacher Hires, Selected Years, Fall 1955 through Fall 2023," National Center for Education Statistics, https://nces.ed.gov/programs/digest/d13/tables/dt13_208.20.asp.

9. "Public and Private school comparison," Fast Facts, National Center for Education Statistics, https://nces.ed.gov/fastfacts/display.asp?id=55.

10. National Center for Education Statistics, Fast Facts: Teacher Trends http://nces.ed.gov/fastfacts/display.asp?id=28.

11. Matthew M. Chingos, "Who Profits from the Master's Degree Pay Bump for Teachers?" SERIES: The Brown Center Chalkboard No. 69 of 115, June 5, 2014, www.brookings.edu/research/papers/2014/06/05-masters-degree-pay-bump-chingos.

12. Wenglinsky, "Private High Schools"

13. Table 24: "Percentage of Kindergartners through Fifth-Graders Whose Parents Were Involved in Education-Related Activities, by Selected Child, Parent, and School Characteristics: 1999 and 2003," National Center for Education Statistics, https://nces.ed.gov/programs/digest/d08/tables/dt08_024.asp.

14. Amber Noel, Patrick Stark, and Jeremy Redford, "Parent and Family Involvement in Education, from the National Household Education Surveys Program of 2012" Washington, DC: National Center for Education Statistics, 2015 http://nces.ed.gov/pubs2013/2013028rev.pdf.

15. The NCES classifies public school students two ways, by those who chose their public school and those who go to designated public schools. Because the latter category encompasses an overwhelming majority—and the stats looked similar—it's the one used. Private school students are classified into religious and nonreligious. Those who go to religious schools make up an overwhelming majority, so I reported that number.

16. Noel, Stark, and Redford, Parent and Family Involvement in Education.

17. "PISA 2012 Results: Students and Money; Financial Literacy Skills for the 21st Century," vol. VI (OECD Publishing, 2014), www.oecd.org/pisa/keyfindings/PISA-2012-results-volume-vi.pdf.

CHAPTER 5

1. "Childhood Obesity Facts," Centers for Disease Control and Prevention, www.cdc.gov/healthyyouth/obesity/facts.htm.

2. Scott Tong, "Middle-Class Parents Weigh the Cost of Getting Their Kids Ahead," Marketplace, June 14, 2013, www.marketplace.org/topics/sustainability/consumed/middle-class-parents-weigh-costs-getting-their-kids-ahead.

3. Jessica Hundley, "Patrice Wilson of Ark Music 'Friday' is on His Mind," Pop & Hiss (blog), Los Angeles Times, March 29, 2011, http://latimesblogs.latimes.com/music_blog/2011/03/patrice-wilson-of-ark-music-friday-is-on-his-mind.html.

4. Jean M. Twenge, PhD, Generation Me: Why Today's Young Americans Are More Confident, Assertive, Entitled—and More Miserable Than Ever Before (New York: Atria, 2014).

5. David Wallechinsky and Amy Wallace, "Celebs Who Sang in Choirs," The Column of Lists, The Victora Advocate, May 26, 1991, http://news.google.com/newspapers?id=f1NSAAAAIBAJ&sjid=rjYNAAAAIBAJ&pg=3459%2C5378704.

CHAPTER 6

1. Barbara Haumann, "American Appetite for Organic Products Breaks through $35 Billion," Organic Trade Association, www.ota.com/news/press-releases/17165.

2. "Three Companies Barred from Advertising Mattresses as Free from Volatile Organic Compounds without Scientific Evidence to Back Up Claims," Federal Trade Commission, FTC File No. 122 3129. The complaint was settled without EcoBaby admitting wrongdoing.

3. United States Department of Agriculture, "What Is Organic." http://www.ams.usda.gov/publications/content/what-organic.

4. Ibid.

5. United States Department of Agriculture National Organic Program, "2010–2011 Pilot Study: Pesticide Residue Testing of Organic Produce" Washington, DC: Agricultura Marketing Service, November 2012.

6. W. A. Knoblauch, R. Brown, and M. Braster, "Organic Field Crop Production: A Review of the Economic Literature" (Ithaca, NY: Cornell University, 1990).

7. Marcin Baranski, et al, "Higher Antioxidant and Lower Cadmium Concentrations and Lower Incidence of Pesticide Residues in Organically Grown Crops: A Systematic Literature Review and Meta-Analyses," *British Journal of Nutrition* 115, no. 4 (September 2014), 794-811.

8. Crystal Smith-Spangler, MD, MS, et al, "Are Organic Foods Safer or Healthier Than Conventional Alternatives, A Systematic Review," *Annals of Internal Medicine* 157, no. 9 (September 2012).

9. A. Mukherjee, D. Speh, E. Dyck, and F. Diez-Gonzalez, "Preharvest Evaluation of Coliforms, *Escherichia Coli, Salmonella* and *Escherichia Coli* O157:H7 in Organic and Conventional Produce Grown by Minnesota Farmers," Journal of Food Protection 67, no. 5 (May 2004):894–900.

10. Miles McEvoy, "Organic 101: Can GMOs Be Used in Organic Products?," USDA Blog, United States Department of Agriculture, May 17, 2013, http://blogs.usda.gov/2013/05/17/organic-101-can-gmos-be-used-in-organic-products/.

11. Fair Trade Resource Network, "What Is Fair Trade," www.organicconsumers.org/sites/default/files/What%20is%20Fair%20Trade_0.pdf.

12. "The Language of Recycling," Federal Trade Commission, www.consumer.ftc.gov/articles/0203-language-recycling.

13. "Shopping Green," Federal Trade Commission, www.consumer.ftc.gov/articles/0226-shopping-green.

14. Nicole Vincent, "Have You Been Bamboozled?" Federal Trade Commission Blog, January 4, 2013, www.consumer.ftc.gov/blog/have-you-been-bamboozled.

15. "FTC Approves Final Order Settling Charges That Tested Green Environmental Certifications Were Neither Tested, Nor Green," Federal Trade Commission, press release, March 1, 2011, www.ftc.gov/news-events/press-releases/2011/03/ftc-approves-final-order-settling-charges-tested-green.

16. "Shopping Green," Federal Trade Commission.

17. "Lawsuit Seeks to Block EPA's 'Free Pass' on Nanosilver," Natural Resources Defense Council, press release, January 26, 2012, www.nrdc.org/media/2012/120126.asp.

18. "FTC Approves Final Orders Settling Charges against the Sherwin-Williams Co. and PPG Architectural Finishes Inc.; Issues Enforcement Policy Statement on 'Zero VOC' Paint Claims," Federal Trade Commission, press release, March 6, 2013, www.ftc.gov/news-events/press-releases/2013/03/ftc-approves-final-orders-settling-charges-against-sherwin.

19. "Three Companies Barred," Federal Trade Commission.

20. "Down to Earth Designs, Inc. Settles FTC Charges That Its Environmental Claims for Diapers and Related Products Were Deceptive," Federal Trade Commission, press release, January 17, 2014, www.ftc.gov/news-events/press-releases/2014/01/down-earth-designs-inc-settles-ftc-charges-its-environmental.

21. "Dioxins and their effects on human health," Fact Sheet No. 225, World Health Organization, updated June 2014, www.who.int/mediacentre/factsheets/fs225/en/.

22. "NRDC: Dangerous Chemical in Soaps and Toothpaste Facing Closer Scrutiny," Natural Resources Defense Council, press release, December 16, 2013, www.nrdc.org/media/2013/131216.asp.

23. Stephen P Luby, MD, et al, "Effect of Handwashing on Child Health: A Randomized Controlled Trial," The Lancet 366, no. 9481 (July 16, 2005): 225–33, doi: http://dx.doi.org/10.1016/S0140-6736(05)66912-7

24. "Bottled Water: Pure Drink or Pure Hype?" Natural Resources Defense Council, last revised July 15, 2013, www.nrdc.org/water/drinking/bw/exesum.asp.

25. Visit the website of the Database of State Incentives for Renewables & Efficiency (www.dsireusa.org) to find the policies and incentives in your state.

CHAPTER 7

1. "Questions and Answers on Dietary Supplements," US Food and Drug Administration, www.fda.gov/Food/DietarySupplements/QADietarySupplements/ucm191930.htm.

2. "Homeopathy: An Introduction," NIH National Center for Complementary and Integrative Health, last updated April 2015, https://nccih.nih.gov/health/homeopathy.

3. Herman Avner Cohen, MD, et al, "Effect of Honey on Nocturnal Cough and Sleep Quality: A Double-blind, Randomized, Placebo-Controlled Study," Pediatrics 130, no. 3 (September 2012): http://pediatrics.aappublications.org/content/early/2012/08/01/peds.2011-3075.full.pdf+html.

4. James A. Taylor, MD, "Echinacea Not Effective in Treating Colds in Children," Journal of the American Medical Association, December 3, 2003.

5. "Homeopathy: An Introduction," National Center for Complementary and Integrative Health.

6. "Press Release, US: Terra-Medica Issues Voluntary Nationwide Recall of Specified Lots of Pleo Homeopathic Drug Products Due to the Potential for Undeclared Penicillin," US Food and Drug Administration, March 30, 2014, www.fda.gov/Safety/Recalls/ucm389832.htm.

7. "Ear Candles: Risk of Serious Injuries," US Food and Drug Administration, updated September 5, 2013, www.fda.gov/Safety/MedWatch/SafetyInformation/SafetyAlertsforHumanMedicalProducts/ucm201108.htm.

8. "Kava," MedlinePlus, US National Library of Medicine, last updated February 15, 2015, www.nlm.nih.gov/medlineplus/druginfo/natural/872.html.

9. "Homeopathy: An Introduction," National Center for Complementary and Alternative Medicine, updated May 2013, https://nccih.nih.gov/sites/nccam.nih.gov/files/Backgrounder_Homeopathy_05-23-2013.pdf.

10. Karine Spiegel, PhD; Rachel Leproult, BS; and Eve Van Cauter, PhD, "Impact of Sleep Debt on Metabolic and Endocrine Function," *The Lancet* 354, no. 9188 (October 23, 1999): 1435–39.

11. "2006 Sleep in America Poll: Highlights and Key Findings," National Sleep Foundation, http://sleepfoundation.org/sites/default/files/Highlights_facts_06.pdf.

12. "Sleep-Wake Cycle: Its Physiology and Impact on Health," National Sleep Foundation, 2006, http://sleepfoundation.org/sites/default/files/SleepWake-Cycle.pdf.

13. "AAP Issues New Guidelines on Treating Ear Infections in Children," American Academy of Pediatrics, February 25, 2013, www.aap.org/en-us/about-the-aap/aap-press-room/pages/AAP-Issues-New-Guidelines-on-Treating-Ear-Infections-in-Children.aspx.

14. Susan S. Lang, "A Room with a View Helps Rural Children Deal with Life's Stresses, Cornell Researchers Report," *Cornell Chronicle*, April 24, 2003, www.news.cornell.edu/stories/2003/04/room-view-helps-rural-children-deal-stress.

15. Caroline Chen, "Surprise Medical Bills Lead to Protection Laws: Health," *BloombergBusiness*, April 4, 2014, www.bloomberg.com/news/articles/2014-04-04/surprise-medical-bills-lead-to-protection-laws-health.

16. "The Affordable Care Act: Patients' Bill of Rights and Other Protections," *Families USA*, April 2011, http://familiesusa.org/product/affordable-care-act-patients-bill-rights-and-other-protections.

CHAPTER 8

1. Leaf Van Boven, "Experientialism, Materialism, and the Pursuit of Happiness," Review of General Psychology 9, no. 2 (2005): 132–42, doi: 10.1037/1089-2680.9.2.132.

2. Ibid.

3. Marsha L. Richins and Lan Nguyen Chaplin, "Material Parenting: How the Use of Goods in Parenting Fosters Materialism in the Next Generation," *Journal of Consumer Research Inc.* 41, no.6 (April 2015): 1333–57, doi: 10.1086/680087.

4. James E. Burroughs, et al, "Using Motivation Theory to Develop a Transformative Consumer Research Agenda for Reducing Materialism in Society," *Journal of Public Policy & Marketing* 32, no. 1 (Spring 2013): 18–31.

5. Lan Nguyen Chaplin and Deborah Roedder John, "Interpersonal Influences on Adolescent Materialism: A New Look at the Role of Parents and Peers," *Journal of Consumer Psychology* 20, no.2 (April 2010): 176–84, doi: 10.1016/j.jcps.2010.02.002.

6. Van Boven, "Experimentalism," 2005.

7. Michael I. Norton, et al, "Prosocial Spending and Well-Being: Cross-Cultural Evidence for a Psychological Universal," *Journal of Personality and Social Psychology* 104, no. 4 (2013): 635–52, doi: 10.1037/a0031578, www.apa.org/pubs/journals/releases/psp-104-4-635.pdf

8. Richard Tunney, "Happiness Comes Cheap—Even For Millionaires," *ScienceDaily*, (December 3, 2007), www.sciencedaily.com/releases/2007/11/071130224158.htm.

9. Chris Manolis and James A. Roberts, "Subjective Well-Being among Adolescent Consumers: The Effects of Materialism, Compulsive Buying, and Time Affluence," *Applied Research in Quality of Life* (2011), doi: 10.1007/s11482-011-9155-5.

10. Keith Wilcox, Lauren G. Block, and Eric M. Eisenstein, "Leave Home without It? The Effects of Credit Card Debt and Available Credit on Spending," *Journal of Marketing Research* 48, Special Issue on Consumer Financial Decision Making (November 2011): S78-S90.

11. "Vehicle Repossession," Federal Trade Commission, November 2008, www.consumer.ftc.gov/articles/0144-vehicle-repossession.

12. "Coping with Debt," Federal Trade Commission, November 2012, www.consumer.ftc.gov/articles/0150-coping-debt.

CHAPTER 9

1. Stacy Berg Dale and Alan B. Krueger, Estimating the Payoff to Attending a More Selective College: An Application of Selection on Observables and Unobservables, Working Paper 7322 (Cambridge, MA: National Bureau of Economic Research, 1999), www.nber.org/papers/w7322.pdf.

2. Stacy Dale and Alan B. Krueger, Estimating the Return to College Selectivity over the Career Using Administrative Earnings Data, Working Paper 17159 (Cambridge, MA: National Bureau of Economic Research, 2011), www.nber.org/papers/w17159.pdf.

3. Anthony P. Carnevale, Ban Cheah, and Andrew R. Hanson. "The Economic Value of College Majors" (Washington, DC: Georgetown University Center on Education and the Workforce, 2015), https://cew.georgetown.edu/wp-content/uploads/Exec-Summary-web-B.pdf.

4. University of Illinois at Urbana-Champaign, "10 Years On, High-School Social Skills Predict Better Earnings Than Test Scores," ScienceDaily (October 16, 2008), www.sciencedaily.com/releases/2008/10/081015120749.htm.

5. Jay Zagorsky, "You Don't Have to Be Smart to Be Rich," ScienceDaily (April 25, 2007), www.sciencedaily.com/releases/2007/04/070424204519.htm.

6. Meta Brown and Sydnee Caldwell, "Young Student Loan Borrowers Retreat from Housing and Auto Markets," Liberty Street Economics (blog), Federal Reserve Bank of New York, April 17, 2013, http://libertystreeteconomics.newyorkfed.org/2013/04/young-student-loan-borrowers-retreat-from-housing-and-auto-markets.html.

7. Charles P. Blahous III and Robert D. Reischauer, A Summary of the 2014 Annual Report, Social Security, www.ssa.gov/oact/trsum.

SELECTED TITLES FROM SEAL PRESS

Spent: Exposing Our Complicated Relationship with Shopping, edited by Kerry Cohen. $17, 978-1-58005-5123. In Spent, editor Kerry Cohen opens the closet doors wide to tales of women's true relationships with shopping, from humorous stories of love/hate relationships with the mall to heartbreaking tales of overspending to fix relationships.

Brokenomics: 50 Ways to Live the Dream on a Dime, by Dina Gachman. $16, 978-1-58005-5673. Through stories both painfully honest and laugh-out-loud funny that anyone can relate to, Dina Gachman shares the lessons she's learned about how to live large in the cheap seats.

The Sh!t No One Tells You About Toddlers, by Dawn Dais. $16, 978-1-58005-5895. Second in the Sh!t No One Tells You series, Dawn Dais tells it like it is—again—offering encouragement, real advice, and a strong does of humor for parents on the edge.

Otherhood: Modern Women Finding A New Kind of Happiness, by Melanie Notkin. $17, 978-1-58005-5710. Melanie Notkin reveals her own story as well as the honest, poignant, humorous, and occasionally heartbreaking stories of women in her generation—women who expected love, marriage, and parenthood, but instead found themselves facing a different reality.

Frientimacy: How to Deepen Friendships for Lifelong health and Happiness, by Shasta Nelson. $16, 978-1-58005-6076. Exploring the most common complaints and conflicts facing female friendships today, Nelson lays out strategies for overcoming these pitfalls to create deeper, more supportive relationships.

Maxed Out: American Moms on the Brink, by Katrina Alcorn. $16, 978-1-58005-5239. Weaving in surprising research about the dysfunction between the careers and home lives of working mothers, as well as the consequences to women's health, Katrina Alcorn tells a deeply personal story about trying to "have it all," and what comes after.

Find Seal Press Online
sealpress.com
@sealpress
Facebook | Twitter | Instagram | Tumblr | Pinterest